At Issue

Animal Experimentation

Other Books in the At Issue Series:

At Issue

Animal Experimentation

Ronnie D. Lankford, Jr., Book Editor

GREENHAVEN PRESS
A part of Gale, Cengage Learning

GALE
CENGAGE Learning™

Detroit • New York • San Francisco • New Haven, Conn • Waterville, Maine • London

GALE
CENGAGE Learning·

Christine Nasso, *Publisher*
Elizabeth Des Chenes, *Managing Editor*

© 2009 Greenhaven Press, a part of Gale, Cengage Learning.

Gale and Greenhaven Press are registered trademarks used herein under license.

For more information, contact:
Greenhaven Press
27500 Drake Rd.
Farmington Hills, MI 48331-3535
Or you can visit our Internet site at gale.cengage.com

For product information and technology assistance, contact us at

Gale Customer Support, 1-800-877-4253
For permission to use material from this text or product, submit all requests online at www.cengage.com/permissions

Further permissions questions can be emailed to permissionrequest@cengage.com

Articles in Greenhaven Press anthologies are often edited for length to meet page requirements. In addition, original titles of these works are changed to clearly present the main thesis and to explicitly indicate the author's opinion. Every effort is made to ensure that Greenhaven Press accurately reflects the original intent of the authors. Every effort has been made to trace the owners of copyrighted material.

Cover photograph © Images.com/Corbis.

LIBRARY OF CONGRESS CATALOGING-IN-PUBLICATION DATA

Animal experimentation / Ronnie D. Lankford, Jr., book editor.
   p. cm. -- (At issue)
  Includes bibliographical references and index.
  ISBN 978-0-7377-4280-0 (hardcover)
  ISBN 978-0-7377-4279-4 (pbk.)
  1. Animal experimentation. 2. Animal experimentation--Moral and ethical aspects. 3. Animal rights. I. Lankford, Ronald D., 1962-
  HV4915.A636 2009
  179'.4--dc22
                                           2008049402

Printed in the United States of America
1 2 3 4 5 6 7 13 12 11 10 09

Contents

Introduction

Millions of animals are used for experimentation each year, from the familiar white mice to the humanoid primates. Because of the sheer number of animals and frequent accusations of cruelty by opponents of experimentation, the issue has become quite controversial. In the midst of heated debates, however, it is easy to become confused over why the tests are being conducted and which organizations are conducting the experiments. For instance, both medical research facilities and cosmetics companies conduct animal experiments, though the purpose behind each is quite different. And both government agencies and private industry conduct experiments, though the government also frequently supports research by private industry and universities.

In order to better understand the issues involved in animal experimentation, it is helpful to be aware of different kinds of research conducted on animals and the kinds of organizations that engage in testing.

Types of Animal Experimentation

- Pure or Basic Research—pure research studies how the biology of animals develops and operates. Unlike other kinds of animal experimentation, pure research is not aimed at specific results. Instead, scientists believe that by knowing more about how animal's brains, bodies, nervous systems, and so on, grow and function, the better they will be able to understand how these systems operate in humans. While research such as the study of memory in animals may have no immediate practical use, it may nonetheless gather scientific knowledge that leads to applications later. Since the cells of animals share many qualities with the cells of humans, animals serve as useful models for pure research.

• Applied Research—unlike pure research, applied research has a specific goal. Scientists study and attempt to find a cure for a specific disease, such as Parkinson's, malaria, or cancer. As with pure research, it is partly based on the similarities between human cells and those of animals. Because leukemia and AIDS appear naturally in felines, for instance, applied research has looked for potential cures by testing new drugs on the immune systems of cats. Biomedical research has also conducted animal experiments with overweight cats because they develop the same diabetes—Type 2—as humans do. Through applied research, medicines and methods are pursued for the practical purpose of eventually treating human diseases.

• Toxicology Testing—toxicology, or safety, testing is conducted by pharmaceutical, cosmetic, and chemical companies. The United States, for instance, requires the testing or the issue of potential-hazard warnings for pharmaceuticals, pesticides, cosmetics, and food additives. While these tests serve a specific purpose—to make certain that a product meets legal safety guidelines before it is marketed—a number of toxicology tests remain controversial. The Draize eye irritancy test is commonly used by the cosmetic industry. The test begins by placing the product in an albino rabbit's eyes and then observing the results for a number of days. No anesthesia is used. Toxicology testing for food products and drugs require lengthier periods of research to make sure that these products have no lasting side effects that might lead to birth defects, cancer, or other problems.

Organizations and Animal Experimentation

- Private Industries—common private industries that utilize animal research include pharmaceuticals and cosmetics companies, but extend to many other industries. Food additives, pesticides, and common household cleaners, for instance, must be tested before they can be legally marketed (the results are overseen by the Food and Drug Administration and other federal agencies in the United States). Also included within the private sector are breeding laboratories (which are in the business of selling test subjects) and contract animal testing facilities (which complete the necessary experiments for other companies). While private companies frequently focus on toxicology testing, some companies have also initiated more open research. For instance, most scientists agree that tobacco products cause health related illnesses, but tobacco companies may wish to gain a broader understanding of how the product causes disease. This, potentially, may lead to products that reduce the risk of illness.

- Governments—a number of government agencies in the United States, including the Environmental Protection Agency, the National Toxicology Program, and the National Institutes of Health, conduct animal experiments. The National Toxicology Program, for example, conducts toxicology tests on household, lawn care, and personal care products. While federal agencies may conduct tests that are similar to those conducted by private industry, the government research helps determine whether any restrictions should be applied on the use of a product. At the beginning of 2008, a number of federal agencies were attempting to find new testing methods that reduced or eliminated the use of animals. The implementation of the program, however, was expected to take ten years.

- Public-Private Partnerships—a number of organizations, in government, private industry, and charitable foundations, provide grants for animal research. Frequently, these organizations are interested in granting money for specific projects (for example, the American Cancer Society provides grants for cancer research) and these grants often require the grantees to follow a number of guidelines. Perhaps the most common partnership traditionally has been the grant money provided for research at universities. In a sense, medical schools, universities, and research facilities provide the expertise, while government and private companies provide the necessary funding.

The Future of Animal Experimentation

These various types of experimentation and various parties conducting the experiments complicate the issue of animal experimentation considerably. For instance, one may find it easy to condemn the use of felines for experimentation within the cosmetics industry, but more willing to accept these experiments when seeking a cure for diabetes. Likewise, one may accept that medical experiments might be necessary but nonetheless object to the use of primates in these experiments. In another instance, one might be skeptical of the need for some types of research when a profit motive is involved, but less so when state or federal governments pursue the same research. With these various complications and interrelationships, the issue of animal experimentation seems likely to remain both complex and controversial for the foreseeable future.

1

Animal Experimentation Is Ethical

Stuart W.G. Derbyshire

Stuart W.G. Derbyshire is a senior lecturer in psychology at the University of Birmingham in England.

In animal research, a consensus has formed regarding the Three Rs: refinement, reduction, and replacement. By reducing the number of animals used in research and relying on alternative testing methods, scientists can look forward to a future of animal-free testing. The Three Rs, however, have been disastrous for science. Animal experiments have advanced (and continue to advance) human welfare, and it is imperative that scientists be allowed to continue their work unimpeded. The Three Rs leave the impression that many experiments on animals have been unnecessary when these experiments have served as essential links in the cure of human disease. Since animal experimentation will continue to be necessary, the scientific commitment to the Three Rs should be brought to an end.

The best hopes to treat or cure any number of diseases all rely on current animal experiments. Like all science, the investigations that scientists perform with animals increase our knowledge of nature and can therefore increase the possibilities for human action, advancing the cause of human freedom. So why do scientists persist in denigrating their own behavior by advocating the three Rs: refinement, reduction, and replacement?

Stuart W.G. Derbyshire, "Time to Abandon the Three Rs," *The Scientist*, vol. 20, February 2006, p. 23. © 2006 Scientist Inc. Republished with permission of Scientist Inc., conveyed through Copyright Clearance Center, Inc.

In the United Kingdom, since the passage of the 1986 Animals (Scientific Procedures) Act, researchers must obtain a license from the Home Office, which involves an assessment of the invasiveness of the study and the species used, following the principles of the three Rs. Invariably, licensing will require considerable justification for any procedures that involve distressing the animal, and considerable pressure will be applied for the use of fewer animals, and from further down the phylogenetic tree (such as using rats rather than primates). Although legislation is less stringent in the United States, in practice the three Rs are still enforced by Institutional Animal Care and Use Committees, which voluntarily assess any proposed research with respect to the three Rs and provide assurance to grant-awarding bodies that the research is animal welfare-friendly.

The impression is that research animals are a necessary evil, when in fact they are just necessary.

Downside of the Three Rs

Through a variety of voluntary and enforced mechanisms, therefore, animal researchers pledge to uphold the three Rs. At first blush, that seems reasonable, if somewhat patronizing. All animal experimenters have an incentive to reduce the amount of stress an animal is subjected to—through refinement—because a stressed animal will be less likely to behave or respond normally and might therefore skew results. Equally, all researchers will naturally tend to use fewer or less-costly animals or techniques—through reduction and replacement—in order to get quicker results for fewer resources.

The three Rs, however, are much worse than patronizing; they are disastrous. They draw attention away from the value of experimentation and toward the importance of animal welfare. By extension, animal experimentation will be looked upon negatively because no animal experiment is in the interests of animal welfare. Adoption of the three Rs comes across as a confession of guilt. The impression is that research animals are a necessary evil, when in fact they are just necessary.

The three Rs also raise false expectation that animals will eventually be replaced as experimental test subjects, which is highly unlikely. [In 2005], in the United Kingdom alone, 2.85 million scientific tests on animals were performed. More, not less, animal research will likely be required to investigate burgeoning models of genetic disease.

Animal Experimentation Is Necessary

Ultimately, we cannot have it both ways. It is not possible to advocate animal welfare and at the same time give animals untested drugs or diseases, or slice them open to test a new surgical procedure. The three Rs encourage a focus on animal welfare that is both unrealistic and dishonest. Regardless of any beliefs about the value of animals, if you engage in activities that are invasive or lethal to animals or if you control their reproduction, their living space and their habits, you are expressing a de facto belief that animals are sufficiently different from humans to make such activities justifiable. Scientists are keen to defend themselves against accusations of cruelty by promoting their allegiance to the three Rs but forget that the real reason for animal experimentation is to advance the welfare and understanding of humanity. Advancing human understanding requires the freedom to do more animal research, and often with higher species, and is incompatible with continued support for the three Rs.

Those of us who research on animals or support that research have made a moral choice to put humans first. We should behave and argue with a conviction that is worthy of the choice. Animal experimentation is a positive activity that advances our appreciation of nature and disease, and defending animal research should be part of a moral campaign that celebrates human knowledge and understanding. Simultaneously advocating animal research while trying to apologize and introduce alternatives is a poor defense of animal experimentation. Successful promotion of animal research can only begin when we withdraw support for the three Rs.

2

Animal Experimentation Is Not Ethical

Animal Friends Croatia

Animal Friends Croatia promotes the protection of animal rights and presents vegetarianism as an ethical way of living.

Estimates of the number of animals used each year for experiments in United States laboratories range from 17 to 70 million. These animals are obtained in a variety of ways, from breeding services to the kidnapping of pets. A number of these experiments are paid for by agencies like the National Institutes of Health and Department of Defense in the United States. Besides causing animals pain, animal experimentation is bad science. In the past, drugs that have proven "safe" for animals have proven harmful to humans. In some cases, relying on animal research has delayed the development of useful medicines. Today there are testing alternatives that are more accurate, making animal experimentation more unnecessary that ever.

Vivisection, the practice of experimenting on animals, began because of religious prohibitions against the dissection of human corpses. When religious leaders finally lifted these prohibitions, it was too late—vivisection was already entrenched in medical and educational institutions.

Estimates of the number of animals tortured and killed annually in U.S. laboratories diverge widely—from 17 to 70 million animals. The Animal Welfare Act requires laboratories

"Vivisection/Animal Experimentation: Sadistic Scandal," *Animal Friends Croatia*, accessed June 23, 2008. People for the Ethical Treatment of Animals. www.peta.org. Reproduced by permission.

to report the number of animals used in experiments, but the Act does not cover mice, rats, and birds (used in some 80 to 90 percent of all experiments). Because these animals are not covered by the Act, they remain uncounted and we can only guess at how many actually suffer and die each year.

Obtaining Animals for Experiments

The largest breeding company in the United States is Charles River Breeding Laboratories (CRBL) headquartered in Massachusetts and owned by Bausch and Lomb. It commands 40–50 percent of the market for mice, rats, guinea pigs, hamsters, gerbils, rhesus monkeys, imported primates, and miniature swine.

Since mice and rats are not protected under Animal Welfare Act regulations, the United States Department of Agriculture (USDA) does not require that commercial breeders of these rodents be registered or that the USDA's Animal and Plant Health Inspection Service (APHIS) inspect such establishments.

Charities, such as the American Cancer Society and the March of Dimes, use donations from private citizens to fund experiments on animals.

Dogs and cats are also used in experiments. They come from breeders like CRBL, some animal shelters and pounds, and organized "bunchers" who pick up strays, purchase litters from unsuspecting people who allow their companion animals to become pregnant, obtain animals from "Free to a Good Home" advertisements, or trap and steal the animals. Birds, frogs, pigs, sheep, cattle, and many naturally free-roaming animals (e.g., prairie dogs and owls) are also common victims of experimentation. At this writing, animals traditionally raised for food are covered by Animal Welfare Act regulations only minimally, and on a temporary basis, when used in, for example, heart transplant experiments; but they are not covered at all when used in agriculture studies.

Unfortunately, vivisectors are using more and more animals whom they consider less "cute," because, although they know these animals suffer just as much, they believe people won't object as strenuously to the torture of a pig or a rat as they will to that of a dog or a rabbit.

Paying for Pain

The National Institutes of Health (NIH) in the United States is the world's largest funder of animal experiments. It dispenses seven billion tax dollars in grants annually, of which about $5 billion goes toward studies involving animals. The Department of Defense spent about $180 million on experiments using 553,000 animals in 1993. Although this figure represents a 36% increase in the number of animals used over the past decade, the military offered no detailed rationale in its own reports or at Congressional hearings. Examples of torturous taxpayer-funded experiments at military facilities include wound experiments, radiation experiments, studies on the effects of chemical warfare, and other deadly and maiming procedures.

Private institutions and companies also invest in the vivisection industry. Many household product and cosmetics companies still pump their products into animals' stomachs, rub them onto their shaved, abraded skin, squirt them into their eyes, and force them to inhale aerosol products. Charities, such as the American Cancer Society and the March of Dimes, use donations from private citizens to fund experiments on animals.

Agricultural experiments are carried out on cattle, sheep, pigs, chickens, and turkeys to find ways in which to make cows produce more milk, sheep produce more wool, and all animals produce more offspring and grow "meatier."

Bad Science

There are many reasons to oppose vivisection. For example, enormous physiological variations exist among rats, rabbits, dogs, pigs, and human beings. A 1989 study to determine the carcinogenicity of fluoride illustrated this fact. Approximately 520 rats and 520 mice were given daily doses of the mineral for two years. Not one mouse was adversely affected by the fluoride, but the rats experienced health problems including cancer of the mouth and bone. As test data cannot accurately be extrapolated from a mouse to a rat, it can't be argued that data can accurately be extrapolated from either species to a human.

In many cases, animal studies do not just hurt animals and waste money; they harm and kill people, too. The drugs thalidomide, Zomax, and DES were all tested on animals and judged safe but had devastating consequences for the humans who used them. A General Accounting Office report, released in May 1990, found that more than half of the prescription drugs approved by the Food and Drug Administration between 1976 and 1985 caused side effects that were serious enough to cause the drugs to be withdrawn from the market or relabeled. All of these drugs had been tested on animals.

Patients waiting for helpful drugs and treatments could be spared years of suffering if companies and government agencies would implement the efficient alternatives to animal studies.

Animal experimentation also misleads researchers in their studies. Dr. Albert Sabin, who developed the oral polio vaccine, cited in testimony at a congressional hearing this example of the dangers of animal-based research: "[p]aralytic polio could be dealt with only by preventing the irreversible destruction of the large number of motor nerve cells, and the work on prevention was delayed by an erroneous conception of the nature of the human disease based on misleading experimental models of the disease in monkeys."

Healing Without Hurting

The Physicians Committee for Responsible Medicine reports that sophisticated non-animal research methods are more accurate, less expensive, and less time-consuming than traditional animal-based research methods. Patients waiting for helpful drugs and treatments could be spared years of suffering if companies and government agencies would implement the efficient alternatives to animal studies. Fewer accidental deaths caused by drugs and treatments would occur if stubborn bureaucrats and wealthy vivisectors would use the more accurate alternatives. And tax dollars would be better spent preventing human suffering in the first place through education programs and medical assistance programs for low-income individuals—helping the more than 30 million U.S. citizens who cannot afford health insurance—rather than making animals sick. Most killer diseases in this country (heart disease, cancer, and stroke) can be prevented by eating a low-fat, vegetarian diet, refraining from smoking and alcohol abuse, and exercising regularly. These simple lifestyle changes can also help prevent arthritis, adult-onset diabetes, ulcers, and a long list of other illnesses.

It is not surprising that those who make money experimenting on animals or supplying vivisectors with cages, restraining devices, food for caged animals (like the Lab Chow made by Purina Mills), and tiny guillotines to destroy animals whose lives are no longer considered useful insist that nearly every medical advance has been made through the use of animals. Although every drug and procedure must now be tested on animals before hitting the market, this does not mean that animal studies are invaluable, irreplaceable, or even of minor importance or that alternative methods could not have been used.

Dr. Charles Mayo, founder of the Mayo Clinic, explains, "I abhor vivisection. It should at least be curbed. Better it should be abolished. I know of no achievement through vivisection, no scientific discovery, that could not have been obtained without such barbarism and cruelty. The whole thing is evil."

Dr. Edward Kass, of the Harvard Medical School, said in a speech he gave to the Infectious Disease Society of America: "[I]t was not medical research that had stamped out tuberculosis, diphtheria, pneumonia and puerperal sepsis; the primary credit for those monumental accomplishments must go to public health, sanitation and the general improvement in the standard of living brought about by industrialization."

3

Pro and Con Positions Oversimplify Animal Experimentation Issues

Jonathan Wolff

Jonathan Wolff is a professor and head of the Philosophy Department at University College, London.

The "pro" and "con" positions on animal experimentation have proven suitable for stating extreme opinions, but unhelpful at exploring the broader ethical questions of animal based research. While there are multiple accusations of animal cruelty, few people actually witness the inner workings of a research lab. Multiple regulations prevent animal cruelty, but animal research still continues to cause pain. Contradictions, however, abound. While an emphasis has been placed on avoiding pain in animal research, a "painless" death—where the rat or rabbit, under anesthesia, is euthanized following the test—is accepted as every day procedure. The use of animals in experimentation raises a number of disquieting moral questions that are difficult to answer definitively. The only hope is that science will continue to evolve, developing new testing methods that will not require the use of animals.

Public moral debates often follow the rules of trench warfare. Two sides face each other behind tangled rolls of barbed wire, guns pointing, insults flying. Each claims to be certain that its cause is the just one, yet neither has an inkling of how to advance. Instead, they just increase the volume.

Jonathan Wolff, "Killing Softly," *Guardian*, March 28, 2006. Reproduced by permission of the author.

The current controversy about the ethics of research involving animals is taking this form. The pros—including the recent student protesters in Oxford—and the antis—which may well include their classmates—both claim to occupy the moral high ground. But, in reality, they are digging themselves deeper into the mire.

When six men became seriously ill in a clinical drugs trial, we were again reminded that questions concerning the science and ethics of animal testing are far from settled. It was to bring more clarity to such debates that the Nuffield council on bioethics [intended to identify and examine ethical questions pertaining to medical research] set up a working party on research involving animals. I was a member of this group, which represented a wide spectrum of views.

Its report contained a set of measures to help those who wish to know more about the realities of animal experimentation, including the provision of more meaningful statistics from the Home Office. This is essential if the debate is to move to a more informed level. There is a moral debate to be had, but not entirely the one we are used to.

The Realities of Animal Experimentation

One of the difficulties is that very few people have direct experience of what actually goes on in animal labs. There is no alternative to relying on second-hand information, such as photographs issued by anti-vivisection groups. Peter Singer, in his famous book *Animal Liberation*, described experiments conducted in the 1970s in which dogs repeatedly suffered severe electric shocks just to see what would happen, and infant monkeys were subjected to various forms of maternal deprivation and abuse, in the hope of gaining insight into the causes of (human) juvenile delinquency. Yet who can be sure whether any of this represents the reality of current research?

Animal ethics had not been a major area of research for me, and my scientific career ended tragically early, owing to my inability to produce a decent drawing of a test-tube. Consequently, I had a lot of catching up to do, which included visiting labs where experiments on animals were taking place. I was not exactly looking forward to this.

The regulatory framework treats animal pain with great seriousness.

I was taken to university and pharmaceutical labs, as well as a contract research facility. All the animals I saw were kept in far better conditions than those in the smelly pet shop where I had recently purchased a hamster. It was a world away from the battery chicken farm I worked on as a teenager. I was surprised by how orderly everything looked. I saw much less pain and suffering than I was expecting. Of course, it would be naive to generalise from the few things I witnessed, and perhaps there would have been a different story to tell if we had stepped into different buildings.

The vast majority of research involving animals in UK laboratories needs to be licensed as it may, and often does, cause pain and suffering. Vaccine research requires infecting animals with some very nasty conditions. Genetic engineering can create animals destined for misery and, of course, some experiments can be done only if the animals suffer pain. Testing the efficacy of painkillers is an obvious example. Nevertheless, regulations require researchers and technicians to keep suffering to a minimum. In cases where it cannot be avoided, experimenters must find ways of keeping pain as mild as possible, and as short-lived.

A Painless Death

Those campaigning for an end to animal suffering in science don't seem to realise quite how well they are doing, on the whole. The regulatory framework treats animal pain with great seriousness.

On the other hand, as I read, saw, and understood more, it was hard to come to the conclusion that when the last lab rat suffers no more pain, all the moral questions will have been answered.

Let me describe one procedure that, I understand, is widely used. It involves "anaesthesia without recovery" and, therefore, no pain or suffering. In these experiments, the researchers attempt to understand the effect a compound will have on an animal's system. The animal, typically a rat or a rabbit, is dosed with anaesthetic to knock it out, and fitted with two catheters: one to keep the dose of anaesthetic topped up, the other to deliver the compound being tested.

The animal is then cut open and pinned out on the bench. Electrodes are placed to detect such things as changes in blood pressure or kidney function. The observations can continue for some hours. When the procedure is completed, the dose of anaesthetic is increased to bring about a "humane endpoint", that is, a painless death.

The curious thing about this example is that while pain and suffering are almost entirely avoided, the death of the animal seems to be of no consequence, at least as far as the current regulations are concerned. Animal pain is taboo; animal death is all in a day's work.

Animal Experiments and Morality

This pattern is repeated elsewhere. Most toxicity testing is performed on mice and rats, but beagles and monkeys are also used. Opinions differ about how much these animals suffer during testing. But every single mouse, rat, monkey or beagle used for toxicity testing will be dead within a few weeks or months, painlessly "euthanised" so a post mortem can be conducted to check whether the drug has affected their internal organs.

Furthermore, animals that have not been experimented on but are killed by humane methods do not have to be counted in the statistics on the number of animals used in research, which the Home Office publishes annually. This would include animals killed for use of their tissue.

It would be foolishly optimistic to think moral arguments alone will bring everyone into agreement.

If there are moral questions to be raised about the procedures I have described, these appear to go beyond a concern with pain and suffering. One reason for feeling disquiet might be based on a belief that every animal is valuable in itself, and so taking its life is morally problematic. Many people will reply that an animal life does not matter in itself; all that matters is what happens to the animal during its life.

Another question is whether it is right for human beings to use animals for their purposes or whether this amounts to a morally unacceptable form of exploitation. Some will say it depends on the human purposes: serious medical research is quite different from sport, say.

The holy grail would be the ability to achieve all of our scientific purposes without using any animals at all.

Changing Scientific Practice

It would be foolishly optimistic to think moral arguments alone will bring everyone into agreement. There is more than one moral position that can be honestly and consistently held on this issue. To say this is not to endorse moral relativism— for it may well be that one of the competing positions is correct—but simply to accept the limitations of moral argument.

The debate needs to continue in a more informed fashion. Follow-up activities organised by the Nuffield council to disseminate the findings of the report, engage with stakeholders and monitor policy developments will continue for a number of years. One important area where the debate could be enhanced is among young people. The council is working with the Nuffield Curriculum Centre to develop resources that will help teachers conduct discussions on this topic.

In practical terms, probably the best we can do is try to evolve scientific practice so that increasing numbers of people will find it less and less objectionable. Progress has already been made. In the UK, for instance, no licence will be granted to allow experiments on the great apes, such as chimps and baboons.

Experiments Without Animals

The holy grail would be the ability to achieve all of our scientific purposes without using any animals at all. Some animal scientists, in academia and industry, are clearly committed to this goal and some are putting their energies into finding alternative methodologies. A national centre was set up in 2004 to pursue the "3Rs": refinement (less suffering), reduction (fewer animals) and, most difficult of all, replacement (no use of living animals).

The Nuffield council report recommends aiming to increase the funding and energy with which alternatives are pursued, and to embed the 3Rs more deeply into scientific education and culture. It may be a fantasy to think we will reach a point where there is no longer any scientific reason to use animals, but it is easy to see why such a goal is compelling. And who, after all, can say what could be achieved by a rising generation of experimenters properly schooled not only in the scientific issues, but the moral issues, too?

4

Dissection Teaches Students Lessons in Cruelty

People for the Ethical Treatment of Animals (PETA)

People for the Ethical Treatment (PETA) of Animals operates under the principle that animals are not ours to experiment on and educates the public about animal abuse.

While many people accept the dissection of frogs and other animals in the biology classroom as a fact of life, classroom dissection is a cruel practice that students should protest. Teaching young adults to ignore the pain of the animals they dissect may reduce the student's ability to empathize with the pain of others. Fortunately, students who believe that dissection is cruel are refusing to take part in the process. While some public schools have offered resistance, many are allowing students the right to not dissect. Luckily, there are a number of alterative methods to experimentation that do not require animals, including computer programs simulating animal biology.

Dissection is the practice of cutting into and studying animals. Every year, millions of animals are dissected in elementary, secondary, and college science classes. Each animal cut open and discarded represents not only a life lost, but also a part of a trail of animal abuse and environmental havoc.

Suppliers

Frogs are the most commonly dissected animals below the university level. Other species used include cats, mice, rats, worms, dogs, rabbits, fetal pigs, and fish. The animals might

People for the Ethical Treatment of Animals (PETA), "Factsheet: Dissection: Lessons in Cruelty," *PETA*, accessed June 23, 2008. Reproduced by permission.

come from breeding facilities that cater to institutions and businesses that use animals in experiments, or the animals might have been caught in the wild—they could also be stolen or abandoned companion animals. A PETA undercover investigator at one of the nation's largest suppliers of animals used for dissection was told by his supervisor that some of the cats killed there were companion animals who had "escaped" from their homes. Slaughterhouses and pet stores also sell animals and animal parts to biological supply houses.

Many students are taking a stand against dissection before it happens in their classes.

PETA investigators documented cases of animals who were removed from gas chambers and injected with formaldehyde without first being checked for vital signs (a violation of the Animal Welfare Act). (Formaldehyde is a severely irritating caustic substance that causes a painful death.) Investigators videotaped cats and rats who were struggling during injection and employees spitting on the animals. One rabbit, still alive after being gassed, tried to crawl out of a wheelbarrow full of water and dead rabbits. Employees laughed as a coworker held the rabbit's head under the water and pulled him out just as death seemed near, repeating the process until, bored with the "game," the employee held the animal's head under long enough to drown him.

Compassion Dies with the Frog

Classroom dissection desensitizes students to the sanctity of life and can encourage students to harm animals elsewhere, perhaps in their own backyards. Serial killer Jeffrey Dahmer attributed his fascination with murder and mutilation to classroom dissections. In the last interview before his death, televised on *Dateline NBC*, Dahmer stated, "In ninth grade biology class, we had the usual dissection of fetal pigs. I took home the skeleton. Started branching out with dogs, cats—I suppose it could have turned into a normal hobby like taxidermy, but instead it became this. I don't know why. It became a compulsion." According to Dahmer, he enjoyed the excitement and power he experienced when cutting up animals and fantasized about cutting up a human body.

Students with little to no interest in pursuing a career in science don't need to see real organs to understand basic physiology. Those students who plan to pursue a career in biology or medicine would do better to study humans in a controlled, supervised setting or to study human cadavers, and there are plenty of other sophisticated alternatives, such as those provided by computer models, to using animals. In further support of these alternatives, students who are disturbed by the prospect of cutting up animals will be too distracted to learn anything of value during the dissection.

Students Speak Up

Many students are taking a stand against dissection before it happens in their classes.

"You don't learn anything about an animal by cutting it up," said Laurie Wolff, a Las Vegas grade school student who successfully petitioned the Clark County School Board to draft a student-choice amendment, providing students with alternatives to dissection. "It's a waste when there are so many other ways to learn about science without having to kill something first," she added. Baltimore student Jennifer Watson, who was taken out of an honors class when she asked for an alternative to cat dissection but allowed back in after a protest prompted officials to reveal that she was entitled to an alternative, explained her actions simply: "I've loved animals my whole life. I was standing up for what I believe in." Ashley Curtis failed a lab exercise in her Minnesota school when she refused to come to class on the day when dissection was scheduled. She said, "I don't think any animals should go through any suffering for education."

The curriculum director of Santa Fe's Public Schools, where a ban on dissection is under consideration, said, "There is really no reason in this day and age to carve up animals. I support [the students] actually."

Most non-animal tools and lessons last for many years and cost less than maintaining a constant supply of animals.

Nearly a dozen states, including Virginia, New York, Pennsylvania, Florida, and California, along with numerous school districts, have enacted laws or policies protecting a student's right not to dissect. Animal dissection has been banned in Argentina, Israel, and India.

Alternatives to Dissection

The typical science lab at many schools now emphasizes computer simulations, interactive CD-ROMs, films, charts, and lifelike models rather than animal cadavers.

Students and teachers may choose from a wide range of sophisticated alternatives to dissection:

- *DissectionWorks* comprises five interactive, computer-dissection simulations, including those of a frog, crayfish, perch, and fetal pig. A digital cat dissection with detailed graphics and information is also available.

- *The Digital Frog* is a fully interactive CD-ROM that allows students to explore the frog through three seamlessly linked modules—dissection, anatomy, and ecology.

- *Body Works* offers a fascinating computer program that explores the body's systems, structure, and functions.

- *Sniffy, the Virtual Rat* is a unique computer program that allows students to explore the principles of operant psychology using a "virtual rat."

- *CatLab* is a fully interactive, multimedia dissection of a cat.

- *Great American Bullfrog* is a large-scale model with numbered parts and a key card. Circulatory, reproductive, and other systems can be separately dissected.

- *Biology Chart Series* includes detailed charts of a dissected frog, perch, crayfish, grasshopper, earthworm, etc.

Many books also offer humane science lessons. *The Anatomy Coloring Book, The Zoology Coloring Book* and *From Guinea Pig to Computer Mouse: Alternative Methods for a Progressive, Humane Education* are appropriate for high school and college students.

Most non-animal tools and lessons last for many years and cost less than maintaining a constant supply of animals. Because computer methods allow students to learn at their own pace, they have proved to be as good as, and often superior to, dissection as a learning tool. One university professor who compared students using an interactive "frog" computer program with those cutting up real frogs found that students using the virtual program learned anatomy just as thoroughly—in an environment that didn't reek of formaldehyde or require killing a living being. Even the vice president of one of the country's largest animal supply companies conceded, "Dissection is no longer cutting edge." . . .

Whether you are a student, a parent, or a concerned taxpayer, you can act to end dissection in your town's school system. If you are expected to perform or observe a dissection, talk to your teacher as early as possible about alternative projects.

5

Animal Experimentation Is Necessary to Ensure Product Safety

PIR Partners Research

Partners in Research (PIR) is a Canadian national charity established in 1988 to educate the public—particularly young people—about the history and accomplishments of health research.

Animal testing has aided humans in a number of important ways. Because of toxicity testing, for instance, poison centers are able to aid parents when a child has swallowed a harmful product. Before animal testing, humans served as the first test subjects for new drugs; because of multiple accidents, however, the government eventually required drug companies to test new products on animals. Scientists have worked to limit the number of animals used in experiments; alternative testing methods have also helped reduce the number of animals used. But the complexity of human biology makes it impossible at present to eliminate animal testing. Until effective technology is available, animal testing will remain a valuable aid to ensuring the safety of new drugs.

Toxicity testing on animals has been invaluable in helping prevent a parent's worst nightmare: the death of a child by accidental poisoning. Most poison control centers have access to a database that lists ingredients and treatments for

"Product Safety Testing," *PIR Partners Research*, accessed June 21, 2008. Reproduced by permission.

most medicines and consumer products. Information on the effects of the products—compiled through toxicity testing on animals—allows treatment to be administered immediately at home.

A parent whose child swallowed a certain type of cleanser, for example, can phone a poison control center for immediate instructions rather than rushing the child to an emergency room. In effect, knowledge gained from toxicity testing has made possible a response that saves money as well as lives.

Before the use of animal testing to determine the harm that might be caused by a drug or product, humans actually served, unwittingly, as the first test subjects. The results were sometimes tragic. An antibacterial sulfa drug was first marketed as a liquid in 1937. The untested formula was made with ethylene glycol (antifreeze) because sulfa drugs do not dissolve well in water. At the time, manufacturers did not need to prove that new drugs were safe to use before they were sold. The compound killed 107 people. The next year, the Food, Drug and Cosmetic Act was passed after a woman was blinded using an eyelash dye.

As useful as "alternative" methods have proven to be, each has limitations.

The Demand for Safe Drugs

Because of this act, and the safety precautions that it entailed, similar mistakes have been avoided. The thalidomide tragedy, in which a drug prescribed to combat nausea in pregnant women caused birth defects in 10,000 European babies, was largely avoided in North America because federal health and drug agencies believed thalidomide had not been adequately tested on animals.

Consumers demand and have a right to expect that the products they depend upon are safe if used properly. They

33

also need reassurance that physicians can save victims in case of accident. Currently, the only way to guarantee these protections is through knowledge gained from animal testing.

No responsible researcher takes a casual attitude toward the use of animals in product safety testing. The well-being of laboratory animals is important to the success of the test procedure. Pain and fear trigger complex hormonal and neurological processes which can alter physiologic response and invalidate test results. Therefore, a distressed animal is a poor test subject.

Although every possible measure is taken to limit the number of animals used and to find new testing methods, replacement of animals entirely is impossible at present. Even those scientists most actively involved in the search for and development of non-animal techniques concur that animal testing must continue. The unthinkable alternative is to risk human safety and human lives. . . .

Alternatives Are Limited

The scientific community has been successful in reducing the number of animals used in safety testing, as well as in refining test methods to reduce any pain or distress these animals may experience. As useful as "alternative" methods have proven to be, each has limitations.

Mathematical models can help to predict an organism's responses to varying levels of exposure to a particular substance. They can also help in improving the design of scientific experiments. These models are, however, no substitute for observation of the effects of a substance in a complex, living system.

Computer data banks allow for the reduction of test duplication. They are also useful in the initial evaluation of chemicals slated for further study; unsuitable chemicals can be eliminated from consideration prior to the institution of animal testing. But computers can only process and store existing knowledge, much of which has come from animal studies. Animal testing is needed to expand that knowledge base.

Cells, tissues, and even whole organs obtained from animals and humans can be used for preliminary screening of chemical compounds. They can help identify substances that are so toxic that there is no purpose in continuing to investigate their potential use. However, in vitro tests cannot reveal the effects of a substance on a complex living organism composed of many different organs and systems. In the end, the validity of such tests must be verified by testing on an appropriate intact living organism.

The Complexity of Human Biology

Micro-organisms and lower invertebrates (single-cell organisms such as protozoa and bacteria) are increasingly useful in early screening for toxic effects. However, because of their simple physiology, they shed little light on complex toxicity questions, and thus are less useful in late stages of testing protocols. Invertebrate animals such as insects and mollusks are also useful in preliminary tests, but the results obtained are often too general to be applied to multi-organ system toxicity problems in humans.

The HPB [Health Protection Branch of Health Canada] states "new methods can never totally replace testing in an appropriate animal model. For example, in vitro methods cannot show complex interactions of a chemical in a living being. Indeed the extreme complexity of the biochemical systems in living creatures cannot be duplicated by our current knowledge, nor will it be in the foreseeable future."

For economic and ethical reasons, there is an active commitment to refine existing tests by minimizing animal distress, to reduce animal usage, to replace whole-animal testing, and to search for more of these alternatives. But before any non-animal method can be accepted as an "alternative," its value as a genuine substitute has to be proven or validated. Industry supports both internal and external efforts to develop and evaluate promising nonanimal procedures.

The public may be confused by announcements that some companies do not test their products in laboratory animals, thus providing "cruelty-free" products. Generally, such claims do not present a full picture. Often the ingredients in the product have already been animal tested, or the manufacturer may have purchased a product formulation from a supplier that previously conducted these tests. Almost all products or the chemical compounds that comprise them were previously tested in animals.

Because a given product may not require animal tests is not evidence that testing can be abandoned for all products. New chemicals, new uses of old chemicals, and new mixtures of chemicals must be subjected to toxicity testing so that unsafe products will not be marketed inadvertently.

6

Animal Rights Activists Are Terrorists

New Scientist

New Scientist, *a UK-based magazine, has been reporting on developments in science since 1956.*

By assaulting individuals associated with animal research, protesters have become terrorists. Unfortunately, these personalized attacks are having the desired effect: research is being curtailed. What these terrorists fail to realize is that animal experimentation has benefited—and continues to benefit—humans. While it should be everyone's goal to reduce the number of animals used in experiments, it is, at present, impossible to replicate many tests without the use of animals. In the near future, however, reducing these numbers is the best way to keep frustrated terrorists from becoming even more strident.

"We live in fear." That is how Ian Gibson MP [member of Parliament], chair of the UK's House of Commons select committee on science, describes life as a target of animal rights extremists. Because of his backing for animal experiments, Gibson and his wife have received death threats and routinely check under their car for bombs.

For countries where animal experimentation is not yet a national issue, the UK shows one way the debate can go. Despite having some of the strictest rules in the world governing what can be done to animals in the name of science, it is

"The Fewer the Better," *New Scientist*, vol. 183, August 7, 2004, p. 3. Copyright © 2004 Reed Elsevier Business Publishing, Ltd. Reproduced by permission.

home to a band of vicious activists. Not content with terrorising researchers, they have taken to threatening shareholders and employees of drug companies—and even firms that do business with those drug companies.

Effective Protests

The victims of animal terrorism describe protests outside their homes, excrement on their doormats and leaflets sent to neighbours alleging they are paedophiles. In one case, protesters showed up at a school attended by the sons of a drug company director carrying a banner calling the boys "puppy killers".

Sadly, these tactics work. In January [2007], the University of Cambridge shelved plans to build a neuroscience research centre that would have used primates. [In July 2007], a construction firm pulled out of a contract to build an animal research centre in Oxford after its offices were vandalised and company shareholders received threatening letters.

After much dithering, the government promised changes in the law to crack down on intimidation. It plans to give police powers to stop protests outside peoples' homes and make convictions for harassment easier. These powers send the right message, though extremists are unlikely to be deterred, simply because they already set out to break the law.

Animal Experiments Necessary

If animal researchers working legally deserve protection, so too do animals, and the case for animal experimentation should be constantly reviewed. The ultimate goal, which the UK government accepts, must be a way of creating new drugs without testing them on large numbers of animals.

So what would happen if, as the more extreme activists demand, animal testing were stopped today? According to the Association of the British Pharmaceutical Industry, nearly 4000 drugs are being tested on animals in the UK. Of these,

89 per cent will be discarded before they get to human trials chiefly because they are toxic to animals. Without animal screening, these tests would have to be done on people. If every drug was tested on, say, 250 people before proper clinical trials began, companies would need a million people to take part. Of these, hundreds are likely to die. Some tests, such as removing organs to look for side effects, would be impossible in humans. Drug discovery would grind to a halt.

> *Only when [the number of animal experiments] begins to fall will anyone feel that progress is being made. If not, frustration will surely feed the ranks of extreme activists.*

How then should government move forward? One way is to seize the initiative. In May [2007], science minister David Sainsbury announced plans for a national centre to explore ways of reducing the number of animals used in experiments. As soon as the centre finds alternatives to animal tests, the government should adopt them in its licensing requirements for drugs and other chemicals.

That said, the number of animals used for experimentation will never fall to zero. Fields such as neuroscience and functional genomics rely heavily on animals. And there are no substitutes for a working brain or genome on the horizon. So long as scientists in these fields have sound justifications for their work, they should be allowed to continue. The alternative is to shut down these disciplines, which would cut off the flow of basic knowledge that will underpin future therapies.

The Animal Testing Dilemma

Ultimately, society has to deal with the central dilemma of animal testing: should animals have the same rights as humans? Campaigners say they should, many scientists disagree. Poll after poll shows that the British public, though it does not like animal tests, takes a pragmatic view: the life of a child always comes before the life of an animal.

For now, the way forward for scientists and government is clear: find alternatives to animal experiments and implement them. The annual number of "procedures" performed on animals in the UK has hovered around 2.7 million since 1995. Only when that number begins to fall will anyone feel that progress is being made. If not, frustration will surely feed the ranks of extreme activists.

7

Animal Rights Activists Are Not Terrorists

Steven Best and Richard Kahn

Steven Best is a University of Texas-El Paso professor, writer, and activist; Richard Kahn writes for the No Compromise Web site.

Animal organizations have learned to wage effective campaigns against corporations that conduct animal research, campaigns that have cost corporations both money and their reputations. While these organizations have restricted their methods of protest to legal means, both the United States government and a number of corporations have struck back. Corporate leaders have asked for new legislation that would define animal activists as terrorists and inflict stricter penalties. In essence, however, the suggested legislation would limit the First Amendment Rights of animal rights protesters. Recent arrests and suggested legislation, then, represent a bold attempt by corporations and the government to limit the civil rights that form the bedrock of democratic protest.

Since 1999, Stop Huntingdon Animal Cruelty (SHAC) activists in the U.K. and U.S. have waged an aggressive direct action campaign against Huntingdon Life Sciences (HLS), an insidious animal testing company notorious for extreme animal abuse (torturing and killing 500 animals a day) and for having manipulated research data. SHAC roared onto the historical stage by combining a shrewd knowledge of the law, no-

Steven Best and Richard Kahn, "Trial By Fire: The SHAC7 and the Future of Democracy," *No Compromise*, vol. 25, Fall 2004, p. 9. Reproduced by permission.

nonsense direct action tactics, and a singular focus on one corporation that represents the evils of the entire vivisection [animal experimentation] industry.

From email and phone blockades to raucous home demonstrations, SHACtivists have attacked HLS and pressured over 100 companies to abandon financial ties to the vivisection firm. By 2001, the SHAC movement drove down HLS stock values from $15/share to less than $1/share.

Growing increasingly powerful through high-pressure tactics that take the fight to HLS and their supporters rather than to corrupt legislatures, the SHAC movement poses a clear and present danger to animal exploitation industries and the state that serves them. Staggered and driven into the ropes, it was certain that SHAC's opponents would fight back. Throwing futile jabs here and there, the vivisection industry and the state teamed up to mount a major counterattack.

War Against Domestic Terrorism?

On May 26, 2004, a police dragnet rounded up seven prominent animal rights activists in New Jersey, New York, Washington and California. Hordes of agents from the FBI, Secret Service, and other law [enforcement] agencies stormed into the activists' homes at the crack of dawn, guns drawn and with helicopters hovering above. Handcuffing those struggling for a better world, the state claimed another victory in its phony "war against terror."

The "SHAC 7" are Kevin Jonas, Lauren Gazzola, Jacob Conroy, Darius Fullmer, John McGee, Andrew Stepanian and Joshua Harper. The government has issued a five-count federal indictment that charges each activist, as well as SHAC USA, with violations of the 1992 Animal Enterprise Protection Act, the first federal law that explicitly seeks to protect animal exploitation industries from animal rights protests.

Additionally, SHAC USA, Jonas, Gazzola, and Conroy were each charged with conspiracy to stalk HLS-related employees across state lines, along with three counts of interstate stalking with the intent to induce fear of death or serious injury in their "victims." All of the charges bring a maximum $250,000 fine each. The main charge of animal enterprise terrorism carries a maximum of three years in prison, while each of the charges of stalking or conspiracy to stalk brings a five-year maximum sentence.

Tellingly, corporate exploiters of animals want to respond to criticism and protest with demands for surveillance, harassment, intimidation, [and] arrests.

The arrests came just over a year after the FBI's domestic terrorism squad raided SHAC headquarters in New Jersey and on the heels of constant surveillance and harassment. Not coincidentally, the round-up also followed shortly after numerous executives from animal exploitation industries appeared before a congressional committee to stigmatize the style of activism practiced by SHAC (and People for the Ethical Treatment of Animals) as a form of terrorism and to plead for new legal measures to counter the increasingly effective direct action tactics of such groups. Following the arrests, Christopher Christie, U.S. Attorney for New Jersey, described the government's intention behind the arrests in dramatically ironic and perverse terms: "Our goal is to remove uncivilized people from civilized society."

Protecting Corporate Interests

The federal indictment against the SHAC 7 is a potential watershed in the history of the animal rights movement, for it represents the boldest governmental attack on activists to date, and it likely augurs a new wave of political repression in response to the growing effectiveness of militant animal liberation politics. Regardless of whether it should win or lose in this proceeding, the corporate-state machine seeks to cast an ominous shadow over activists who dare to exercise their First Amendment rights. Tellingly, corporate exploiters of animals want to respond to criticism and protest with demands for surveillance, harassment, intimidation, arrests and appearances before grand juries.

Little more than a week before the May 26 [2004] raid on the SHAC 7, a phalanx of high-level vivisectors and animal industry representatives marched into the U.S. Senate Committee on the Judiciary to carp about the inadequacy of existing regulations to crush SHAC and other militant animal rights groups.

On May 18, 2004, chair of the Judiciary Committee, Sen. Orrin Hatch (R-UT) took opinions from: U.S. Attorney McGregor Scott; John E. Lewis, FBI Deputy Assistant Director for Counterterrorism; William Green and Jonathan Blum, senior vice presidents of Chiron Corporation (a noxious puppy killer associated with HLS) and Yum! Brands, Inc. (the supersized parent company behind most well-known fast-food chains); and Dr. Stuart Zola, director of the Yerkes Primate Center.

One after another, these motley billion-dollar boys shamelessly tried to cast themselves, their colleagues, and their family members as innocent victims of animal rights hooligans as they appealed for assistance in stopping what they claimed amounts to "terrorism." Indeed, to listen to their combined testimony, the United States of America is a sort of uncontrolled Baghdad or Kabul war zone, besieged by marauding animal militias, rather than a highly-centralized network of power bent on repressing dissent and regulating everyday life for the capital mongers.

Attacking Civil Liberties

The 2001 passage of the USA PATRIOT Act and its vilification of "domestic terrorism" was by no means the first state volley in the war against animal liberation. For over a decade, animal exploitation industries and the state have collaborated to create laws intended to protect corporations and researchers from animal rights activists. In 1992, the federal government enacted the first major law designed to strike at the freedom of protest and dissent, the Title 18 Animal Enterprise Protection Act (AEPA), which contains subsection 43 on "animal enterprise terrorism." The law targets anyone who "intentionally damages or causes the loss of any property (including animals or records) used by the animal enterprise, or conspires to do so." It also seeks to make an offender of whomever "travels in interstate or foreign commerce, or uses or causes to be used the mail or any facility in interstate or foreign commerce for the purpose of causing physical disruption to the functioning of an animal enterprise." Yet, if the corporate-state complex has its way, Sen. Hatch will soon introduce new legislation that will make the legal right to transform the way institutions conduct themselves—through measures such as protests, demonstrations, and boycotts—a felony crime.

William Green of Chiron Corporation typified the whining before the Judiciary Committee when he asked Congress to send a stronger message to animal and earth activists and to open the door to greater surveillance by federal, state, and local officials. Even though Chiron's revenue grew to $1.8 billion in 2003, apparently the $2.5 million in lost earnings caused by SHAC, along with the tarnishing of the corporation's reputation, makes SHAC enough of a threat that biotechnology companies and vivisectors want Congress to gut the Constitution to protect assumed corporate "rights" to profit from animal cruelty and scientific fraud. Thus, Green asked Congress to impose harsh 10-year sentences on the anti-vivisection "terrorists" and to define "animal enterprise" in broader terms that include not only all manner of organizations that use animals, but the non-animal enterprises that contract with these outfits as well.

Fortunately, not everyone in government is moved by the hysterics of the animal research community. The committee's minority leader, Sen. Patrick Leahy (D-VT), refused to even be present for this corporate conspiracy masked as a Senate hearing. Instead, Leahy wrote a statement for the public record that vilified the proceedings, wherein he remarked that ". . . most Americans would not consider the harassment of animal testing facilities to be 'terrorism,' any more than they would consider anti-globalization protestors or anti-war protestors or women's health activists to be terrorists."

Do corporations and the state, as they claim, really respect the First Amendment and the democratic political sensibilities behind it?

As he wondered aloud why not a single animal rights advocate was brought before the committee in a hearing supposedly designed to investigate "Animal Rights: Activism vs. Criminality," Leahy also repeated his request for an oversight hearing with U.S. Attorney General John Ashcroft, who had dodged questioning from the Committee for over a year.

First Amendment Controversies

The key issue for American citizens in the indictment of the SHAC 7 concerns the defendants' First Amendment rights to freedom of speech and association. Critics of direct action protest, such as those who testified before the Senate Judiciary Committee, invariably claim that they respect the right to dissent, distinguishing "legitimate" (and easily contained) expressions of criticism and objection from those involving alleged criminal action. But according to U.S. Attorney Christie, the SHAC 7 defendants were "exhorting and encouraging" actions not protected by the Constitution.

The strategy of the corporate-state is to define SHAC-styled direct action as beyond the scope of constitutional protection. They seek to narrow the meaning of the First Amendment and therefore to subject SHAC and other activists to an increasingly broad scope of criminal prosecution. Key questions, then, emerge from the United States' attempt to prosecute SHAC: Do corporations and the state, as they claim, really respect the First Amendment and the democratic political sensibilities behind it? Are SHAC actions legal or illegal expressions of dissent? And, if they are illegal, do they constitute a special form of terrorism deserving of federal injunction, or are the myriad of extant laws capable of penalizing specific acts of civil disobedience sufficient?

Freedom of speech is the exception, not the rule, of life in the USA.

The latitude of the First Amendment is broad but, as is widely understood, rights are not absolute. The First Amendment does not grant individuals unqualified freedom to say or do anything they desire as a matter of civic right. According to classical liberal doctrine, such as formulated by philosopher-economist J.S. Mill, liberties extend to the point where one's freedom impinges upon the good or freedom of another. Thus, no one has the right to injure, assault, or take the life of another endowed with rights. That, of course, is the theory. In American political practice, restrictions on liberty are frequently applied to consumers and citizens alike, but rarely to corporations who—capitalizing on the predatory logic of property rights—systematically exploit humans, animals, and the environment to their own advantage.

While there have been some strong defenses of the First Amendment by the U.S. Supreme Court, such as the protection of the Ku Klux Klan's use of hate speech, there have also been severe lapses of judgment. Indeed, the entire last century is scarred by egregious Constitutional violations, ranging from the Red Scare of the 1920s, the loyalty oaths of the 1930s, and

Sen. Joseph McCarthy's witch hunts in the 1950s, to the FBI COINTELPRO operations of the 1960s and 1970s, and the passage of the USA PATRIOT Act in 2001. U.S. history is riddled with precedents that demonstrate systematic and sweeping violations of First Amendment rights, such that freedom of speech is the exception, not the rule, of life in the USA.

The Suppression of Dissent

The indictment of the SHAC 7 is just one of many clear indicators that we have entered into yet another chilling period of social repression and the quelling of dissent. While the media have largely focused public attention on [President George W.] Bush's imperial Pax Americana, domestic police and federal agents have violently repressed demonstrations, surveilled legal organizations, collected and disseminated information on activists, and summoned individuals to grand juries in the attempt to intimidate and coerce information. Within this conservative social climate, as people are besieged by monopolistic capitalism, quasi-fascistic patriotism, religious ranting, and cultural paranoia, the corporate-state complex is using SHAC to launch its latest attack upon the Bill of Rights.

Put in this context, SHAC clearly is within its rights to criticize HLS, Chiron and other corporations for exploiting animals. As established in landmark rulings by the Supreme Court, such as *Brandenburg v. Ohio* (1969), the First Amendment grants citizens the right to free speech up to the point of advocating violence toward others in such a way that violent actions might result in an immediate and imminent threat of one's speech. SHAC reports on violent actions taken by individuals under the banner of groups such as the ALF [Animal Liberation Front] or Revolutionary Cells, and it posts home addresses and personal information of HLS employees or affiliates. But SHAC does not advocate violence against anyone, certainly not in any manner that incites immediate and imminent criminal actions.

Moreover, critics never trouble themselves with the crucial distinction between SHAC USA Inc., an aboveground, legal and non-violent organization, and "the SHAC movement," comprised of a wide-range of activists united against HLS that sometimes use illegal tactics and may have an underground presence. In its economically and politically-motivated confusion, the corporate-state complex has targeted SHAC USA Inc. rather than the shadowy SHAC movement.

In *NAACP v. Claiborne Hardware Co.* (1982), the Supreme Court ruled that an organization cannot be held accountable for actions of its members or followers; thus, SHAC USA Inc. is not responsible for the actions of the SHAC movement. To make the state's case against SHAC even more difficult, the Supreme Court ruled in 2003 that anti-abortionists had the legal right to hold home demonstrations against abortion rights advocates, a decision that has clear implications for SHAC's tactics against HLS.

8

Mainstream Animal Rights Groups Support Extremists' Actions

Ed Owen

Ed Owen is a political and communications consultant advising a range of organizations, including those involved in the debate over the use of animals in medical research.

Traditionally, any protest movement has had both moderate and radical groups within its fold. In the contemporary animal rights movement, however, moderates have resorted to the same extremist positions as the radicals. Even moderate animal rights groups dismiss the opinions of the medical community and regularly decry charitable donations given to organizations associated with animal research. These views are also becoming more mainstream, with 25 percent of the general population opposing animal research and a number of politicians adapting "moderate" animal rights rhetoric. While efforts to reduce the number of animals used in experimentation are worthy, the elimination of animal experimentation in the foreseeable future is unrealistic. By suggesting that animal experimentation can be eliminated, moderate animal rights groups are misleading the public and providing cover for extremists.

It is "the ultimate evil" and "the most intense form of systematic cruelty in the history of humanity". Strong stuff. Yet these are not descriptions of the Holocaust or the genocides

Ed Owen, "The Dangers of Cuddly Extremism," *New Statesman*, September 12, 2005. Reproduced by permission.

of Rwanda or Cambodia. It is how one animal rights group chooses to describe on its website the use of animals in scientific research. And far from being members of a balaclava-clad [hooded], extremist fringe, the authors of this rhetoric are from a mainstream organisation called Uncaged, which lobbies the government and works closely with many of our MPs [members of Parliament].

In the wake of the news [in August 2005] that Darley Oaks Farm in Staffordshire [UK], which bred guinea pigs for research purposes, was being forced to shut down its business, there has been a renewed focus on the militants within the animal rights lobby who use intimidation and violence to get their way. But in doing so, we must also step up effective scrutiny of the equally uncompromising arguments of those groups that do act within the law. Make no mistake, these so-called moderate organisations are as fundamental in their aims, if not in the tactics, as the hard core.

I should at the outset declare an interest. My three-year-old daughter suffers from cystic fibrosis, a life-threatening inherited condition that attacks the lungs and digestive system. About one in every 2,500 babies born in the UK is affected. Our refrigerator and kitchen cupboards are full of medicines that have been developed with the help of animal research. Using these treatments, most sufferers can expect to live until their early thirties with a disease that few used to survive beyond childhood.

But every one of us has reason to thank animal research; and its value to medical progress is backed by the overwhelming weight of serious scientific opinion. Only last month [August 2005], 700 scientists, including 500 eminent medical research scientists—in whose number could be found three Nobel laureates, 190 fellows of the Royal Society and the Medical Royal Colleges, and more than 250 professors—signed a declaration affirming this position. Yet that position is dismissed out of hand by the animal rights lobby, and not just by the extremist fringe.

Animal Rights Extremists

The British Union Against Vivisection (BUAV) is one of Britain's oldest and most established groups, with a history of peaceful protest and legitimate activities against animal research. Yet, like every other mainstream group, it does not merely oppose animal experiments on ethical grounds—namely, that whatever the benefits, the subordination of animals' "rights" in support of human beings is always morally wrong (which is at least a logical argument, if not a particularly persuasive one in a nation of animal eaters as well as animal lovers). Rather, it seeks to dispute and often demonise current scientific opinion. "As well as being ethically unsupportable," the BUAV states, "we believe that animal experiments are . . . unreliable [and] are potentially delaying medical progress by focusing research attention and funds on a fundamentally flawed methodology."

This accusation of "bad science"—a favourite phrase of the animal rights lobby—is taken even further by Animal Aid, an organisation that claims to have a list of celebrity supporters including Richard Wilson, Glenda Jackson and Simon Cowell. In its response to the declaration from the 700 scientists, Animal Aid claimed that animal research was not only useless but "a proven hazard to human health". Animal Aid is one of those groups that is critical of many well-known medical charities because of the charities' association with animal research. It says that organisations such as the British Heart Foundation, the National Asthma Campaign, the Meningitis Trust and Cancer Research UK are being "conned". The National Anti-Vivisection Society (Navs), another mainstream, law-abiding group, advises its supporters against giving money to these bodies, which it describes as "the bad guys". Jan

Creamer, Navs chief executive, denies this represents a boycott, but argues that it is designed as a service to its members who wish to know which charities to donate to.

As its description of animal research as "the ultimate evil" suggests, Uncaged is another animal rights organisation that eschews understatement and caution. Its spokesman Dan Lyons justifies Uncaged's rhetoric, but argues that it should be "seen in context". "Obviously, if you look through human history, there have been sporadic moments when humans have committed terrible cruelty on each other," he admits. "But what marks out animal experimentation is its systematic infliction of pain or cruelty on millions of animals every year across the world."

Thus, it should be of little surprise that in its response to the activities of the militant extremists who forced Darley Oaks Farm to cease its involvement in animal research, Uncaged—an organisation that is at pains to proclaim its law-abiding credentials—blamed the government and media for creating what it described as "the underlying causes of anger and frustration" which drove compassionate people to break the law. Lyons said: "Our bottom line is that we are against violence, whether against humans or animals. The statement we issued was a sociological explanation rather than an ethical judgement."

Mainstreaming Radical Views

It is tempting to dismiss this sort of commentary as peripheral—and it is true that some groups such as the BUAV were unequivocal in their condemnation of the tactics used against Darley Oaks. But the emotive and fundamentalist language used by mainstream bodies hardens opinion on this highly contentious issue and, in some quarters, risks providing a respectable cover for those whose activities hover at the margins of legality. Many of the legitimate groups continue to attract support, and although most opinion polls show most people favour the idea of animal research for medical purposes, a [media research firm] MORI survey [in 2000] found that as much as a quarter of the population is opposed to all animal research, regardless of its purpose.

All the law-abiding groups have friends in high places, too. One is Norman Baker, a Liberal Democrat MP and the party's spokesman on animal welfare. He has worked with many of the lobby groups and is quoted on the Uncaged website as saying that it "keeps alive the flame of hope that one day animal experiments will seem as outdated as sending children up chimneys [to clean them] seems today".

An extreme minority has managed to force the closure of a number of establishments connected with animal research and will continue to target others.

Baker disowns the emotive language that Uncaged uses and is clear that he condemns militant activity. However, he backs much of the analysis offered by the mainstream animal lobby. "I believe that we should be getting away from using animals altogether," he told me. "The scientific establishment is conservative, and hanging on to animals in this way is like hanging on to nanny." He believes that alternatives such as the use of computer modelling or cell cultures, and even using human volunteers, would be a far more effective way to pursue medical research, although he accepts that change is not going to happen overnight. "Pragmatic politics suggests that it is easier to nibble at this issue bit by bit. But I believe that we can, and should, end all such experiments over the next 20 years."

Such a pronouncement will amaze most of those involved in medical research. Yet Baker is not the first politician to have flirted with animal rights groups in the hope of winning popular support. Before the 1997 general election, [the] Labour [Party] sought to win over those in favour of an end to animal research with a promise to set up a Royal Commission to consider the issue. The commitment appeared in a glossy leaflet published in 1996 called *New Labour, New Life for Animals*, although wiser heads ensured that it got nowhere near the election manifesto [platform]. The later decision to withdraw the party's pension-fund investment from Huntingdon Life Sciences, a company that has been mercilessly targeted by animal rights extremists, was a huge error of judgement.

Supporting Responsible Experiments

The number of animal experiments has been halved over the past 30 years as a result of tighter legal restrictions and new alternatives to help research. The welfare of the animals used—85 per cent are rats, mice and other rodents—has improved significantly in that time, and in recent years the testing of tobacco and cosmetic products on any animal has been banned. Yet the need for animals to be used in medical research will undoubtedly continue to exist for the foreseeable future. In fact, the numbers of scientific procedures carried out on animals has risen in the past two years as new molecular biology techniques require an increase in the use of genetically modified animals.

Such work holds enormous potential for humankind. Yet if the research is to continue, and the great benefits it offers to be realised then ongoing public support and legitimacy are vital. An extreme minority has managed to force the closure of a number of establishments connected with animal research and will continue to target others. Yet the mainstream groups will be active, too, using legitimate methods to win over people who are rightly concerned about animal welfare. They will continue to use exaggerated and highly charged arguments unsupported by scientific opinion. Those of us who want to see responsible medical research flourish have a duty to ensure their claims are put under the greatest scrutiny. It is within this debate that the vital argument about animal research will be won and lost.

9

Alternative Testing Can Replace Animal Experimentation

Carol Howard

Carol Howard is the communications coordinator at the Johns Hopkins Center for Alternatives to Animal Testing in Baltimore, Maryland.

Because science has relied on animal experimentation for so long, it is difficult for many people to believe that alternative methods can replace traditional testing. But the Three Rs— replacement, reduction, and refinement—offer a promising starting point to reimagine testing methods. Organizations like the Center for Alternatives to Animal Testing (CAAT) have promoted these principles in a variety of ways. CAAT, for example, has provided funds to help develop alternative testing methods and has proven successful at reaching scientific consensus between government agencies and private organizations. While the elimination of animal experimentation may not be possible at present, educating the next generation of scientists on the possibility of alternatives is essential to reaching this goal eventually.

When I first told my father I had gotten a job with the Johns Hopkins Center for Alternatives to Animal Testing, he said, "I don't believe it." Not that he didn't believe I got a job (well, maybe that, too). But my father, an MD/PhD and former dean of a major medical school, didn't believe

Carol Howard, "Yes, Dad, There Are Alternatives," *AV Magazine*, vol. CXIII, Spring 2005, pp. 14–15. Reproduced by permission.

there are alternatives to the use of animals for research and testing purposes. Neither cells grown in a test tube nor computer simulations—nor any manner of non-animal methodology—he argued, can predict the complex interactions that occur within an entire living system.

My father's reaction isn't unusual, especially among scientists and those who work in biomedical fields. His response isn't altogether wrong, either. Not all animal research or testing can be replaced by non-animal methods at this time—and some may never be.

The Three Rs

I explained to him about the "3Rs" of alternatives: replacement, reduction, and refinement. Replacement is what most people think of when you say "alternatives to animal testing"—the animals are replaced, either by methods that don't involve animals at all (mannequins, computer simulations, etc.) or by in vitro (literally, 'in glass') techniques, where the studies are done with cells or tissues in culture.

The other two Rs, reduction and refinement, refer to reducing the number of animals to the minimum necessary for the study and to refining the techniques to eliminate or minimize pain and distress. My father allowed [that] these two certainly were possible, though he grumbled some about referring to them as 'alternatives.' He is not alone in that, either.

The word 'alternatives' has been the source of both confusion and controversy. Many scientists object to the term, arguing that it suggests that all animal research can be replaced, and prefer "adjunct methods." Animal activists may reject any animal use altogether and hence reject reduction and refinement as alternative methods. Some in the alternatives field prefer to call it "humane science."

Furthermore, success has a way of rendering an alternative invisible. For example, not so long ago, pregnancy testing involved killing a rabbit. These days, a woman can buy an over-the-counter kit that tests her urine for a certain hormone. No one thinks of this as an alternative, though clearly an in vitro method has replaced an animal test. This presents something of a double bind: If an alternative method really works and is used regularly, then it's not an alternative. It's simply current practice, best practice.

Establishing Alternative Principles

British scientists William Russell and Rex Burch first delineated the concept of the 3Rs (but did not use the word 'alternatives') in their classic 1959 book, *The Principles of Humane Experimental Technique*. Russell and Burch's systematic study of laboratory techniques pointed to what they call the "intimate relationship between humanity and efficiency in experimentation"—i.e., humane science is the best science.

The Center for Alternatives to Animal Testing (CAAT) is based upon these principles. CAAT works to promote the creation, development, validation, and application of the 3Rs of alternatives in biomedical research, product safety testing, and education. From the outset, the Center has operated three major programs: research grants, workshops/symposia, and information.

Many companies no longer test on animals at all, and those that do use far fewer animals and more humane methods.

CAAT was founded in 1981 with a grant from the Cosmetic, Toiletry and Fragrance Association, with the idea that the Center would work to develop in vitro and other innovative non–whole-animal methods for product safety testing. CAAT's research grant program serves to provide critical seed money for scientists interested in developing alternative methods. To date, the Center has funded some 300 grants for a total of about $6 million. Through this program, CAAT has helped establish the basic scientific knowledge leading to a variety of in vitro methods for evaluating the safety of commercial and therapeutic products.

Achieving Scientific Consensus

Over the intervening 20-plus years, the safety testing of personal care products has changed dramatically. Many companies no longer test on animals at all, and those that do use far fewer animals and more humane methods. This is by no means due entirely to CAAT, but the Center clearly helped lead the way.

In addition to providing funding for new research, CAAT has an unparalleled record for bringing together and achieving consensus among diverse groups with often divergent interests regarding the use of animals in research and testing. For more than 20 years, the Center has been organizing symposia and workshops on the 3Rs of alternatives, bringing together academic and industrial scientists, animal welfare organizations, and the government regulatory community for discussions of common ground.

CAAT's symposium series was so successful that it evolved into the World Congress on Alternatives and Animal Use in the Life Sciences. CAAT proposed and served as host for the first World Congress, held in Baltimore in 1993. The World Congresses have continued, meeting in Utrecht, The Netherlands in 1996; Bologna, Italy in 1999; and New Orleans in 2002. The 5th World Congress [convened] in Berlin, Germany in August 2005. [The 6th was in Tokyo in 2007, and the 7th in 2009 in Rome, Italy.]

CAAT workshops and symposia have helped give rise to significant policy changes. For example, prompted by AAVS's [American Anti-Vivisection Society] campaign to end the use of mice in producing monoclonal antibodies (MAbs), CAAT hosted a workshop addressing this matter in 1997. In response to both these efforts, the National Institutes of Health issued a

'Dear Colleague' letter directing researchers to use in vitro methods for MAb production instead of the ascites method, which involves growing tumors in mice. . . .

Educating the Next Generation

CAAT is part of the Johns Hopkins Bloomberg School of Public Health, and education is an important thread running through all our programs. In fact, education is the key that will make alternatives work over the long haul. In The Netherlands, for example, all biomedical students are required to go through a 3-week intensive program that addresses the proper design of animal experiments, alternative methods, animal welfare issues, and ethical aspects of animal experimentation. The course is designed to make students take a critical attitude toward animal experiments and to help them incorporate the 3Rs into their experimental design.

I look forward to the day when . . . there is no such thing as alternatives. Just humane science, the best science.

Currently [2005], there is nothing comparable in the United States. CAAT has made a start, however. In February 2004, the Center launched an online course on Enhancing Humane Science—Improving Animal Research aimed at students, researchers, and laboratory technicians. The lectures include a range of subjects related to humane science, including in vitro and other replacement approaches, as well as such topics as non-invasive imaging; environmental enrichment; measurement, avoidance and relief of pain and distress; impact of stress on quality of data; and humane endpoints. This course is the first of its kind in the United States and is available free of charge. . . .

If students learn to think in terms of alternatives from the outset, incorporating the 3Rs when they plan experiments, including these concerns in their initial literature search, then it ceases to be some extra burden—it is simply current best practice. The trick is to get these ideas woven into the very fabric of the science they conduct. That is the way to make alternatives work over the long haul. Of course, then they will not be considered "alternatives" any more.

I look forward to the day when my father is right—when there is no such thing as alternatives. Just humane science, the best science.

10

Alternative Testing Cannot Replace Animal Experimentation

George Poste

George Poste is a veterinarian and the director of the Biodesign Institute at Arizona State University.

Alternative testing cannot replace animal experimentation. When animal extremists suggest otherwise, they are 1) being dishonest, and 2) preying on the general public's discomfort with animal experimentation. Governments routinely require that new drugs be tested on animals before they are marketed. Furthermore, replacement tests like computer simulations cannot reproduce the complexity of human genetics. In truth, both corporations and scientists are highly motivated to not use animals in experiments whenever possible: Alternative testing is frequently more cost and time efficient. Extremists, who now rely on terrorist tactics, should not be allowed to set the agenda on animal experimentation. The questions that one asks about the use of animals, whether in experiments or farming, should revolve around ethical treatment.

As a veterinarian and someone who has spent three decades in biomedical research in academia and the pharmaceutical industry, I know that animal research saves lives.

With the announcement of [drug development company] Covance's plans for a major drug development facility in

George Poste, "Animal Testing a Necessary Research Tool, For Now," *Arizona Republic*, September 3, 2006. Reproduced by permission.

Chandler [Arizona], I am concerned by deceptive claims from extremist groups about the need for animal research.

Animal studies continue to be necessary for advancing human and animal health and have played a vital role in virtually every major medical advance. This includes life-saving drugs and vaccines, new surgical procedures and improved diagnosis of disease.

A hallmark of humanity is our ability to care about other species. It is understandably difficult for people to reconcile this empathy with support of animal studies for medical advances that cure disease and improve the quality of life.

Opposition to all animal testing would require a life without drugs, vaccines, painkillers, anesthetics and surgery.

Animal extremists prey on this discomfort and count on society's general lack of scientific insight to advance their agenda. These extremists knowingly misrepresent the ability of computers and emerging scientific techniques to serve as viable substitutes for animal studies.

Animal Research Is Necessary

Government regulations around the world require that new drugs, vaccines and surgical implants first be tested in animals for potential toxic reactions. Beyond these formal legal requirements, research into the root causes of disease at the genetic level and how diseases become resistant to current treatments cannot be simulated by computer programs or duplicated in test tubes.

Although present-day technology cannot yet replace many types of animal research, the research community is committed to finding new ways to reduce and replace animal testing.

This ethical commitment is embodied in strict animal welfare protocols at most university, government and industrial laboratories.

In addition to humane considerations, the economic and logistical advantages of replacing animal testing are compelling. Animal studies are time-consuming and resource-intensive. If meaningful alternatives existed, companies could save hundreds of millions of dollars in facilities and personnel costs.

Opposition to all animal testing would require a life without drugs, vaccines, painkillers, anesthetics and surgery. It would demand a rejection of all federally mandated Food and Drug Administration and Environmental Protection Agency tests that ensure the safe consumption of products in our homes and workplaces, ranging from the testing of components used in computers and cellphones to plastic wraps and chemical additives in our foods and drinks. In short, it would require a lifestyle far removed from that enjoyed by most people, particularly the jet-setting celebrities who oppose animal research.

Need for Ethical Beliefs

Reducing complex issues to oversimplified sound bites encourages the thinking that wearing a lapel ribbon is a substitute for education and dedication to seeking solutions. Research scientists, physicians and veterinarians face tough moral and ethical issues in this pursuit and take these responsibilities seriously.

Concern about animal welfare can take very different forms. Some people are offended by the use of leather and fur as fashion accessories but accept that medical research must unavoidably use animals until viable alternatives are found. Some groups argue persuasively against intensive farming practices but, again, recognize the need for animals in medical research. I recently signed a petition in Arizona calling for reform in the raising of veal calves.

My advice is that people carefully consider not just whether or not a group shares their beliefs, but whether or not they behave in an ethical manner. The tactics used by opponents of Covance in Chandler have included false claims about alternatives to animal testing and misinformation aimed at provoking community concerns about potential disasters.

Well-funded national groups often disguise their involvement to make it appear as if local citizens are leading the effort. In May [2006], *The Arizona Republic* uncovered deceptive methods and use of false names by a leading opponent of the Chandler drug-development facility in an attempt to camouflage ties to People for the Ethical Treatment of Animals and involvement in other protest campaigns.

Animal Rights Extremists

Of greatest concern are those who encourage violence in the name of animal activism. My family and I have been the targets of death threats, as have many of my colleagues. Several animal extremist organizations have been identified by the FBI as serious domestic terrorism threats.

Surveys show that most Americans support the need for animal studies aimed at medical advances.

People for the Ethical Treatment of Animals provides funding to the Animal Liberation Front, which is listed as a terrorist group by the governments of both the United States and the United Kingdom.

A publicly available report from the FBI describes People for the Ethical Treatment of Animals as an organization that "recruits interns for the sole purpose of committing criminal acts."

In 2003, a representative of the Physicians Committee for Responsible Medicine, another national group that has been prominent in the local debate, called for the assassination of doctors whose research involves animals.

Fortunately, very few people endorse such extreme views. Surveys show that most Americans support the need for animal studies aimed at medical advances. Even as divergent as the views of animal activists and researchers may seem to be, there is agreement on one key issue: We all look forward to a day when mankind's ingenuity provides a way to completely eliminate the need for animal studies.

I have a challenge to offer to anyone who feels strongly about this topic, especially young people. If you sincerely wish to eliminate the need for animal research, put down your picket signs, learn about the subject and invent solutions. I guarantee you'll find a receptive audience in the medical research community, because it's a goal we share.

11

Research Funding Is Responsible for Animal Experimentation

National Anti-Vivisection Society

Founded in 1929, the National Anti-Vivisection Society (NAVS) is an educational organization whose ultimate goal is the elimination of animal use in research.

While a convincing case can be made for the ineffectiveness of animal research, scientists continue these experiments unabated. The primary reason, while seldom broached, is fairly obvious: financial incentives have guaranteed the continuation of animal experimentation. Although researchers are often seen as serving a higher scientific purpose, they, like everyone else, must draw a paycheck each week. Many scientists have already built reputations in the field of animal studies, and are disinclined to debunk the basis of a lifetime of work. Medical training also reinforces the belief that animal experiments have been responsible for most scientific breakthroughs. Further conflicts of interest emerge when pharmaceutical companies provide university labs with funds to test new products. In the end, animal experimentation has been, and continues to be, carried out from a lack of knowledge about its true value and greed by large companies.

Anti-vivisectionists use a two-pronged argument to substantiate their case against animal experimentation. They oppose animal experimentation on both ethical and scientific

"Animals in Scientific Research: Medical Research," *National Anti-Vivisection Society*, accessed June 23, 2008. Reproduced by permission. http://www.navs.org.

grounds. Both perspectives of this argument provide compelling testimony that vivisection is cruel and inadequate, and that it wastes time, money and resources that could be better put to use in relieving human suffering.

Why, then, do researchers continue to conduct and defend animal experiments in light of insurmountable evidence, even from within the scientific community, that it provides meaningless results? The answers are many and varied, but they all lead down the same path: money.

Despite the fact that animal experimentation has been shown to be a flawed methodology, animal research continues because it is in the best financial interests of scientists, as well as a number of other entities. These entities include universities, regulation bureaucrats, pharmaceutical companies, scientific journals, animal breeders, lawyers and even the news media. All of them profit, either directly or indirectly, from animal research, and are therefore deeply committed to maintaining the status quo.

Careers Depend on Research

Consider the scientist whose job security and prestige rest upon the number of scientific articles he or she can get published. It's called the "publish or perish" syndrome, and it's alive and well at academic institutions all over the country. It is not the quality of research that's important, but rather the quantity. The more articles a researcher publishes, the more secure his or her position will be. Researchers who don't publish often enough end up untenured or unemployed. And the competition is fierce. Only about 15 percent of all research applications are accepted.

Scientists are often put on a pedestal, exalted for their intelligence and investigative powers. But they too have bills to pay and families to support. It all comes down to financial security and career advancement, and animal experiments provide an efficient route. Unlike clinical research (working with human-based data), animal experimentation generates faster results with less effort. It is estimated that for every one paper a clinician can produce, an animal researcher can produce five. That's because animal research doesn't take as long to produce; animal life spans are much shorter than that of humans, and diseases progress much faster.

Scientists who understand the worthlessness of animal experimentation are quickly silenced.

Often, researchers follow the easiest path of all: taking a concept that's already been established, then "tweaking" it a bit by injecting a variable (such as a different animal species or dosage) to justify an additional study. It's done all the time, and results in an enormous amount of virtually duplicative studies. Moreover, the "concept" often has already been proven using human-based data.

Resistance to Change

Although profit is probably the greatest motive for researchers to conduct animal experiments, it is not the only one. People and society in general are resistant to change. If we have always done something the same way, it is unlikely we will change unless something catastrophic happens to make us change. Many scientists are rooted in tradition, and tradition tells them that animal research is an appropriate method of investigation. Large academic institutions reward convention over innovation, and so creative thinking is generally not welcome in the hallowed halls of science. Those scientists who understand the worthlessness of animal experimentation are quickly silenced. Those who refuse to be silenced do so at great career peril.

Another reason animal experimentation continues is the human ego. People who experiment on animals have published hundreds of papers in the scientific literature. Their entire self-image is that of an animal researcher. If you take away their importance, vis à vis their publications, their self-worth will plummet. Most people will not allow that to happen.

Physicians often support animal research out of sheer habit. They are taught to memorize in medical school, not to think critically or to study the history of their profession. Physicians who work for the vested interest groups such as university hospitals, will maintain the party line as their institutions make millions from animal research each year. There also exists a significant gap between the people who perform animal research, and the clinicians who actually treat your illnesses. The right hand in medicine really does not know what the left is doing. There is a split between what the clinician does, and what he is taught in the first 2 years of medical school by animal researchers.

Spin Control

Most clinicians were taught that all medical breakthroughs came from animal experiments, and they just repeat this throughout their careers. The typical clinician usually does not have, or make, the time to look up where real breakthroughs came from. The private practice physician has probably never questioned animal experimentation—since medical school he has been working long hours, and has not been in a conducive atmosphere for questioning authority.

There is great deal of spin control in medical research. Werner Hartinger, M.D., a surgeon in West Germany, stated in 1989, "There are, in fact, only two categories of doctors and scientists who are not opposed to vivisection: those who don't know enough about it, and those who make money from it."

Some who perform research on animals, mainly researchers with a PhD, are far removed from patient care. They are naïve. Many are very ethical, honest people but because they do not see patients on a daily basis they do not see the disconnect between what they are doing in the lab, and what actually works in the clinics.

The animal tests are used as a quick stepping stone to clinical trials, while providing a legal safety net for the drug companies.

And yet, another reason animal research persists is guilt. More than once we have heard people say, "If what you say is true why have I killed all those animals?" Many people do love animals, including some who experiment on them. They honestly think they are doing the right thing, and if they ever saw otherwise, the guilt they would suffer would be severe.

Follow the Money Trail

Now let's follow the money trail a little farther down the road—to the pharmaceutical companies that also benefit from animal research. When drug companies develop a new compound that has potentially therapeutic effects for humans, they will give large sums of money (in the millions of dollars) to an academic research institution to study the drug. The researchers test the drugs on animals. If the drug passes animal tests, it moves on to clinical (human) trials, and then to the marketplace where it will generate untold profits for the drug companies.

The animal tests are used as a quick stepping stone to clinical trials, while providing a legal safety net for the drug companies. Animal tests are used to prove, or disprove, personal injury claims against drug companies (and the government) that result from unforeseen side effects. Thus, they protect companies from lawsuits which can cost a great deal of money.

In addition to scientists and pharmaceutical companies, animal research puts money into the pockets of biological supply houses that supply animals, as well as the equipment and materials used to maintain them, in laboratories. Most publishers of scientific journals are predisposed to animal experimentation because it provides a steady source of material to publish. They have profited by creating more and more journals, which bring in tremendous revenues from advertising (by drug companies and biological supply houses).

Even as a few benefit from this vast and interrelated web of profit-taking, there are many, many losers. Untold numbers of animals suffer unimaginable fates. Sick people who could benefit from treatments that are delayed by the machine of animal research are, in many ways, as victimized as the animals. And the hard-earned money of the American taxpayer, who foots the bill for the vast majority of animal experimentation through government research grants, is wasted away while far more worthwhile programs remain underfunded or cut due to lack of funds.

Conspiracy is defined as an agreement to perform together an illegal, treacherous or evil act; an agreement between 2 or more persons to commit a crime. *This is not a conspiracy*. Animal research can be explained by the same things that have hurt humans for millennia; greed, ego, ignorance, and fear.

12

Using Primates in Medical Experimentation Is Unjustifiable

Humane Society of the United States

The Humane Society of the United States (HSUS) is the nation's largest animal protection organization.

While animal experiments on chimpanzees have been outlawed in much of the world, the United States continues to use great apes for research. The use of chimpanzees in experiments began in 1920 in the United States, and was expanded by the air force during the 1950s. Since the 1980s, chimpanzees have been used in several types of research, including gene therapy and drug testing. Unfortunately, a number of these tests are ineffective while others cause extreme stress to the animals; furthermore, housing for chimpanzees is often inadequate for the animals' social needs. Luckily, the Chimpanzee Health Improvement, Maintenance and Protection Act has allowed a number of animals to be rescued from research facilities and relocated. While this program has aided a number of chimpanzees, many animals will continue to suffer until great ape research is outlawed and all of these animals are freed.

Approximately 1,200 chimpanzees—some who were captured from the wild, used by the entertainment industry or kept as pets—currently live in nine biomedical research and testing laboratories across the United States. Despite ex-

"Frequently Asked Questions About Chimpanzees in Research," *Humane Society of the United States*, www.humanesociety.org, accessed August 28, 2008. Reproduced by permission of The Humane Society of the United States, www.humanesociety.org.

tensive knowledge of their rich social and emoti
their ineffectiveness as models for human dise
chimpanzees continue to be subjected to painf
experiments—some for over 40 years now. Most chimpa..
aren't being used and end up languishing in laboratories for
decades, wasting taxpayer dollars. It's high time to finally end
this wasteful and poor treatment of our closest living and endangered relatives.

What Is the History of Chimpanzee Research in the United States?

Chimpanzee research in the United States began in the 1920s
when Robert M. Yerkes purchased a chimpanzee and a bonobo
for his home-based laboratory. His research contributed to
some of the first descriptions of chimpanzee behavior and intelligence and an understanding of their similarities to humans. Named after Robert Yerkes and located in Atlanta, Ga.,
Yerkes National Primate Research Center has since shifted its
behavioral studies of chimpanzees to biomedical research, according to a 1995 analysis by the Committee on Animal Models in Biomedical Research.

---

*The majority of chimpanzees in laboratories at any given
time are not being used and are simply being warehoused; often at taxpayer's expense.*

In the 1950s, the U.S. Air Force established a chimpanzee
breeding colony from wild-caught chimpanzees for research to
determine the effects of space travel on humans, which included subjecting the chimps to extreme G forces and electric
shocks as punishment during training. By the 1970s, the Air
Force no longer used chimpanzees, but would lease them out
to facilities for biomedical research. Around this time, the
Convention on International Trade in Endangered Species of
Wild Fauna and Flora was adopted. CITES put severe restric-

tions on importing chimpanzees from the wild. As a result, a federally funded captive breeding program was established so that chimpanzees would be available to research.

Why Should We Give Special Attention to Chimpanzees?

What we know about these animals should serve as a wake-up call. They exhibit a range of emotions including pleasure, depression, anxiety, pain, distress, empathy and grief. Chimpanzees are very social, highly intelligent, and proficient in tool use, problem solving, and numerical skills and can even be taught American Sign Language. But that's not all. Due to the overwhelming evidence of their intelligence and ability to experience emotions so similar to humans, their suffering under laboratory conditions cannot be refuted.

What Is Causing the Recent Decline in the Use of Chimpanzees for Biomedical Research and Testing?

Fortunately, the scientific community and others have decreased the use of chimpanzees both nationally and internationally due to:

- High costs of keeping chimpanzees in laboratories

- Serious ethical concerns

- Unsuitability of chimpanzees as research models for humans

- Public pressure

What Is Life Like for Chimpanzees in the Laboratory?

In the wild, chimpanzees live in very diverse social groups and travel several miles in one day. However, in some research protocols, chimpanzees are forced to live alone in cold, metal cages approximately the size of a closet. Individual housing of chimpanzees can cause severe problems such as depression, heightened aggression, frustration and even self-mutilation. In addition to solitary housing, chimpanzees used in research are often subjected to many painful and distressing procedures including numerous liver biopsies, isolation from others for long spans of time, injection of human viruses, and frequent "knockdowns" in which chimpanzees are shot with a dart gun of anesthetic. It is important to note, however, that the majority of chimpanzees in laboratories at any given time are not being used and are simply being warehoused; often at taxpayer's expense. Even when not being used, the laboratory can cause the chimpanzees anxiety and fear due to seeing other chimpanzees undergo procedures and not knowing what may happen to them next.

Which Laboratories Have Chimpanzees Available For and Used in Invasive Research?

There are currently nine laboratories in the United States which use or house chimpanzees for invasive research purposes. Those labs are:

- Alamogordo Primate Facility (Alamogordo, NM)

- Bioqual, Inc (Rockville, MD)

- Center for Disease Control (Atlanta, GA)

- Food & Drug Administration (Rockville, MD)

- MD Anderson Cancer Center (Bastrop, TX)

- New Iberia Research Center (New Iberia, LA)

- Primate Foundation of Arizona (Mesa, AZ)

- Southwest National Primate Research Center (San Antonio, TX)

Yerkes National Primate Research Center (Atlanta, GA)

Who Pays for Research on Chimpanzees?

U.S. taxpayers spend an estimated $20–$25 million each year on experiments involving chimpanzees, including their care. The estimated expense of simply maintaining one chimpanzee in a laboratory is $20–$39 per day. This high cost works to the chimpanzees' advantage, as it is one reason their use has been declining. The government will save an estimated total of $15 million per year if invasive research is ended and the 600 government-owned chimpanzees are retired to sanctuary.

Is the Public Supportive of an End to Invasive Biomedical Research on Chimpanzees?

Opinion polls indicate growing public concern regarding the use of chimpanzees in biomedical research.

13

Using Monkeys in Medical Experimentation Is Justifiable

Research Defence Society

The Research Defence Society (RDS) is the UK organization representing medical researchers in the public debate about the use of animals in medical research.

Although monkeys are currently used for very few experiments, they remain an important part of neuroscience research. Most monkeys used in research are treated well: they are bred specifically for experimentation and are housed in environments that allow both interaction with other monkeys and participation in normal behavior (foraging, climbing, etc.). The primary reason that monkeys continue to be used in research rests upon the similarity between monkey and human brains. Animal experiments that rely on monkeys allow researchers to better understand how Alzheimer's and Parkinson's disease, along with drug addiction and schizophrenia, affect the human brain. Through experiments with monkeys, scientists have made advances in all of these fields that have greatly benefited humans.

Much of what we know about the human brain comes from neuroscience research on monkeys. Given our present state of knowledge, research on monkeys is likely to be necessary for the foreseeable future. We have too little detail about how the human brain is organised for computer models of the brain to be of great use at this stage. But, where non-animal methods can be used, it is illegal to use animals. It is

"Hot Science: Monkeys and Brain Research," *RDS (Research Defence Society)*, www. rds-online.org.uk, accessed June 23, 2008. Reproduced by permission.

also important to note that our closest cousins, great apes (chimpanzees, gorillas and orangutans), haven't been used in UK research for at least 20 years and their use is now banned.

Monkeys in UK Research

Most research animals are rodents: monkeys are required in less than one fifth of one percent (ie about one in 700) of animal experiments in the UK. Only a fraction of these are used in neuroscience research. When it is necessary to use monkeys, they are normally purpose-bred in approved centres. Although wild-caught monkeys may be used in very exceptional circumstances, this has not happened for several years.

It is now standard practice to house research monkeys in social groups, and to provide them with plenty of space and a stimulating and diverse environments. This means they can carry out their full range of normal behaviour such as foraging for food, climbing, swinging and grooming. As far as possible, pain and distress [are] avoided, for instance by using non-invasive procedures or training monkeys to cooperate with their human carers. Indeed, in most neuroscience studies the active and voluntary participation of the monkey is essential, so it is very much in the interest of the researcher to make the study as rewarding as possible for the monkey.

Why Are Monkeys Used?

Our understanding of the functioning of nerve cells has been based on animals such as the rat and even invertebrates such as squid, but the organisation of these nerve cells to form complex systems in the brain cannot be understood without studying the monkey brain. The complex nature and connectivity of these neural systems in humans is much closer to that found in the monkey brain than in other animals. For example, certain parts of the brain such as the cerebral cortex are poorly developed in other animals. And the temporal and frontal lobes of the cortex, which are involved in functions such as perception, attention, memory and planning in the human brain, are underdeveloped in lower animals.

There is very strong evidence that there are structural, functional, behavioural and neurobiological similarities between humans and monkeys. Research into neurological disorders involving higher functions and brain structures such as the frontal lobes depends much more on studies of monkeys than of other animals. For example, disorders such as depression, schizophrenia, attention deficit hyperactivity disorder (ADHD), autism, drug addiction and obsessive compulsive disorder all involve malfunctioning of the frontal lobes and their interactions with other parts of the brain. This is also true of conditions such as head injury, Parkinson's and Huntington's diseases, stroke and some types of dementia.

Last century, monkeys were essential in the development of the polio vaccine, which has saved millions of lives. In which areas of research are monkeys important today? Here we look at the use of monkeys in understanding how the brain works, and outline research that aims to understand and treat Alzheimer's disease, Parkinson's disease, drug addiction and schizophrenia. Monkeys are also used in research into epilepsy, stroke, autism and blindness, and in areas not related to neuroscience, such as developing safe and effective vaccines for AIDS and malaria, and in transplant research.

Organisation of the Brain

One way in which studies of monkeys have been essential has been their use to determine the detailed 'wiring diagram' of the human brain: how different systems connect to one another. Many brain disorders arise because of loss of communication between different brain regions or are due to impaired function within these regions. It has proved largely impossible to understand the wiring of the human brain from post mortem studies, and studies of rodents are of limited use because their brain structure is not sufficiently similar to that of humans. Structural brain scanning using CT [computed tomography] or MRI [magnetic resonance imaging] cannot determine accurately in space and time how these connections are made. So it is necessary to study the anatomy of the monkey brain at the microscopic level.

Brain and Behaviour

To study how nerve cells work to produce behaviour it is necessary to examine their firing patterns using microelectrodes. This technique does not in any way incapacitate the animal and only causes minimal discomfort (the brain itself does not have pain receptors, so does not feel pain). The techniques are quite similar to those used in certain human disorders such as epilepsy where it is necessary to record brain activity.

Information from monkey studies provides the basis for understanding how brain systems form impressions of the world, make decisions and act appropriately—the process known as cognition. Studies of the human brain using imaging techniques are inadequate for fully understanding the role of the brain in cognition for several reasons:

- the nature and therefore the exact meaning of the images with respect to nerve activity is incompletely understood;

- the resolution of the signals in space and time is not yet good enough;

- it does not establish cause and effect—it only shows that certain systems may be active during cognition.

The most precise way of determining the role of particular brain structures or systems is to study the way they function when they are damaged or temporarily inactivated. In humans, it is difficult to come to definite conclusions about brain-behaviour relationships on the basis of brain damage, because the damage in patients arising from accidental injuries or disease is often diffuse or extends across several different brain regions. Techniques for temporary inactivation of the human brain, such as transcranial magnetic stimulation, have drawbacks. They affect the functioning of an undefined number of active systems and the results may be difficult to interpret.

For studies of cognitive function it is therefore necessary to study the effects of small areas of damage which involve particular brain cells or systems, and this can be achieved in the cerebral cortex and related areas of the brain in monkeys. The damage is normally reversible. For such experiments, it is vital that the animals are stress-free and are kept in good conditions. No forms of painful negative motivation are used, although the monkeys may have to work for some of their preferred foods. In general monkeys enjoy solving puzzles and interacting with computer screens.

Studies of monkeys led to understanding of the entire nerve circuitry involved in human Parkinson's disease.

Alzheimer's Disease

Alzheimer's disease is a devastating disease of old age that causes memory loss, emotional problems and impaired reasoning. It affects one person in 10 over the age of 65 and almost half those over the age of 85. It begins in the temporal lobe and related brain areas.

The development of Alzheimer's disease is thought to be associated with the death of certain brain cells (known as cholinergic cells) due to the build-up of an insoluble protein called amyloid-beta (A-beta) to form white plaques, and the formation of tangles of a second protein, tau, inside the sufferers' brain cells. Brain cells cannot regenerate, probably because of the absence of a substance called nerve growth factor. In monkeys this substance has been shown to prevent the death of brain cells and stimulate connections between them.

It is generally impossible to mimic all aspects of a complex human disorder such as schizophrenia or Alzheimer's disease with animals by producing symptoms that exactly match those of the human disorder. However, it is possible to mimic some aspects and some of the resulting symptoms. For example, damage to parts of the cerebral cortex and hippocampus in monkeys—areas affected by Alzheimer's disease in humans—causes symptoms such as memory loss and can be used to assess novel anti-Alzheimer's drug therapies.

Parkinson's Disease

People with Parkinson's disease (some 120,000 in the UK) suffer from shaking, rigidity, balance problems and slowed movement. Similar symptoms that are a side-effect of other diseases are termed Parkinsonism.

Although Parkinson's disease is probably not naturally present in most animals it is possible to re-create some of the symptoms. In fact, our understanding of Parkinson's disease has depended almost entirely in studies with other animals, principally rodents and monkeys. For example, animal studies were directly responsible for the discovery and measurement of the neurotransmitter dopamine in the brain. Dopamine is deficient in certain parts of the brain in Parkinson's disease. Animal studies have also led to development of the successful therapy, L-dopa. However, L-dopa medication is not a perfect treatment and doctors have been seeking other forms of treatment—based for example on transplanting stem cells into the brain or on other techniques.

One of these is the 'brain pacemaker', or Deep Brain Stimulation (DBS) of the subthalamic nucleus. Studies of monkeys led to understanding of the entire nerve circuitry involved in human Parkinson's disease. Part of the problem in Parkinson's disease is that the loss of dopamine in a region called the basal ganglia causes the output system to seize up because other areas of the brain become too active. Switching off a specific part of the basal ganglia called the subthalamic nucleus can curb these effects. This can be done by stimulating this brain area with tiny amounts of electrical current. This was originally shown to work in monkeys with Parkinson's disease symptoms—and is now being used in human patients with considerable success. The benefits are often immediately apparent and quite dramatic. Over 20,000 Parkinson patients worldwide have now been treated with DBS.

Drug Addiction and Schizophrenia

It is now gradually becoming clear that long-term drug abuse may be associated with brain damage in humans. This may make it impossible to fully rehabilitate addicts, even when they are detoxified. In fact, some difficulties with complex decision-making are linked with the duration of abuse of drugs such as amphetamine. This may also be true for related drugs such as MDMA (ecstasy). However, we do not know the basis of this—it may arise from some pre-existing fault in the brain of the drug abuser. It is impossible to be sure whether the drug abuse has actually caused these problems because we cannot study humans at earlier stages in their development, nor can we ever be fully aware of the variety of drugs or other things that may have affected them. The only way to determine cause and effect is to study this in an experimental, controlled manner in animals.

Recent advances with gene microchip technology are showing that certain genes are expressed differently from normal in the frontal cortex of the brain of patients with schizophrenia. However, it is difficult to be sure whether these potentially important clues to how the brain has become 'miswired' are actually due to a disease process, or possibly arise in brain development, or are merely side-effects of treatment with drugs which are used to treat schizophrenia. The same types of gene are expressed in the monkey frontal lobes. Only by studying whether comparable drug treatments lead to the same changes can we understand what is really causing the changes in gene expression. As well as this need to understand how anti-schizophrenic drugs work, it is becoming increasingly necessary to determine how such drugs may improve the impaired cognitive functions of the temporal or frontal lobes. This impairment prevents full rehabilitation, even after psychotic symptoms have disappeared.

14

Animal Experimentation Is Vital for Medical Research

Foundation for Biomedical Research

The Foundation for Biomedical Research (FBR) is the nation's oldest organization dedicated to improving human and veterinary health by promoting public understanding and support for humane animal research

Animal experimentation has played—and continues to play—a vital role in scientific research. Because there are so many similarities between human and animal physiology, experimentation has allowed scientists to discover new treatments for diseases and guarantee the safety of new drugs. Furthermore, while animal rights extremists have attempted to discount the importance of this research, many scientists and medical societies support it. Animal research has provided the basis for numerous medical innovations, including vaccines, organ transplants, and pacemakers. Whether one focuses on strokes, childhood cancer, or AIDS, animal experimentation has led to improved human health and longevity.

From the discovery of antibiotics, analgesics, antidepressants, and anesthetics, to the successful development of organ transplants, bypass surgery, heart catheterization, and joint replacement—practically every present-day protocol for the prevention, control, cure of disease and relief of pain is based on knowledge attained—directly or indirectly—through research with animals.

Foundation for Biomedical Research, *Proud Achievements of Animal Research*. Washington, DC: Foundation for Biomedical Research, 2008. © 2008 Foundation for Biomedical Research. Reproduced by permission.

Animal [rights] extremists often claim that the results of animal studies can't be applied to human health. However, physicians and researchers overwhelmingly agree that animal systems provide invaluable and irreplaceable insights into human systems because there are striking similarities between the physiological and genetic systems of animals and humans. Since the dawn of medical science, insights drawn from studies with lab animals have been critically important in the design and proper interpretation of human studies. Indeed, studies of human populations and clinical cases could not be interpreted without the basic scientific understanding that came from centuries of research with animals. There is also a legal requirement to test drugs, medical devices, and other promising treatments on animals before they are administered to humans.

The essential need for animal research is recognized and supported by scientists, medical societies, and health agencies around the world. Further proof of its validity can be found in the vast body of Nobel Prize–winning work in physiology and medicine that has been achieved with animal models ranging from fruit flies to zebrafish.

Preventing Disease

In 2006, infant mortality in the USA—a key indicator of the nation's health—was measured at fewer than seven deaths per 1,000 live births compared to 47 deaths per 1,000 live births in 1940. Much of this progress came from knowledge gained through animal research.

Many diseases that once killed millions of people every year are now either preventable, treatable or have been eradicated altogether. Immunizations against polio, diphtheria, mumps, rubella and hepatitis have saved countless lives. Without animal research, these vaccines would not exist. The survival rates for many other major diseases are at an all time high thanks to the discovery of powerful new drugs, the development of new surgical procedures and the design of sophisticated medical devices.

Pacemakers, artificial joints, organ transplants and freedom from arthritic pain are just a few of the breakthroughs made in veterinary medicine thanks to animal research. Dogs, cats, sheep, and cattle also are living longer and healthier lives thanks to vaccines for rabies, distemper, parvo virus (infectious diarrhea), infectious hepatitis, anthrax, tetanus and feline leukemia. And new treatments for glaucoma, heart disease, cancer, hip dysplasia and traumatic injuries are saving, extending and enhancing the lives of beloved companion animals while advanced reproductive techniques are helping to preserve and protect threatened species.

Animal Research Achievements

The following list represents a brief chronicle of the dramatic progress in recent years that has been made in the prevention and treatment of a myriad of diseases. In every case, critical steps in the basic understanding of the disease and knowledge of how to combat it came from animal-based research.

Between 1950 and 2004, U.S. deaths from stroke and heart disease fell by 72 percent and 63 percent, respectively;

Between 1974 and 2001, the overall U.S. five-year survival rate for childhood cancers increased by 29 percent;

Between 1995 and 2005, AIDS-related deaths in the U.S. fell by 70 percent;

Safe and effective vaccines have been developed to control the following common diseases, once regarded as "killers": polio, measles, diphtheria, pertussis (whooping cough), rubella, mumps, tetanus, influenza and pneumococcal pneumonia.

More than 400 million children under the age of five years were immunized against polio during mass vaccination campaigns in 2007. Almost 2 billion doses of vaccine were administered to children in 47 polio-affected and high risk countries. Poliovirus, the causative agent of paralytic poliomyelitis, essentially has been wiped out in North America. Since the World Health Organization (WHO) polio eradication program began in 1988, only four of 125 countries remain endemic for polio—the smallest number in the history of this crippling disease.

A widely prescribed class of drugs known as "statins" can block plaque buildup in arterial walls and reduce the incidence of heart attacks. Newer "statins" with improved efficacy show beneficial secondary effects in the treatment of coronary heart disease, stroke, multiple sclerosis, osteoporosis and Alzheimer's disease.

The accumulation of beta amyloid containing plaques in the brain correlates with the onset and progression of Alzheimer's disease (AD), a disorder characterized by progressive loss of memory and dementia. Researchers are attempting to develop a vaccine that can help the brain destroy plaques and lower their production. New cognitive-enhancing drugs that slow memory decline also are becoming available.

[Thanks to animal research] many different anti-HIV (human immunodeficiency virus) drugs approved for human use have led to dramatic declines in AIDS-related diseases and deaths.

Dramatic improvement in the treatment regimens with novel anti-cancer drugs permits 90.4 percent of American children suffering from acute lymphocytic leukemia to remain in remission for at least five years. These long-term survivors often go on to lead normal lives.

More than 100 million vaccine doses of influenza virus strains are produced annually for the U.S. to prevent outbreaks and reduce the impact of this disease on the national population. Certain strains of influenza can have serious consequences, even death, for high-risk persons, especially children and the elderly.

Thousands of people, particularly young men, suffer acute spinal cord injuries each year as a result of accidents. Scientists are now finding potential new spinal cord therapies to spur neurons to grow and create new connections, enabling recovery of sensations and motor functions. Eventually, paralysis may be reversed.

More than 350 million people around the world are chronic carriers of hepatitis B. This virus can cause long-term, chronic illness that leads to cirrhosis of the liver, liver cancer and death. Hepatitis B virus infections can be prevented by vaccination and controlled by precautionary treatments.

Recent advances in the development of a vaccine for Ebola virus offer hope of controlling this gruesome disease, characterized by hemorrhagic fever, which is almost always fatal.

Some 20.8 million Americans live with (juvenile and adult onset) diabetes. Nearly six million depend on a daily treatment with insulin to control blood sugar. A new array of non-invasive devices to monitor glucose levels, and new needle-free systems to deliver insulin, such as skin patches, sprays, and inhalers, are making life easier for those who live with diabetes. Islet cell transplants hold out hope for a cure of the disease.

Many different anti-HIV (human immunodeficiency virus) drugs approved for human use have led to dramatic declines in AIDS-related diseases and deaths. Newly developed vaccines that protect monkeys from simian AIDS are being tested in clinical trials, giving rise to the hope that a safe and effective human AIDS vaccine will be found to control the virus infection.

Levodopa (L-dopa) provides initial relief from (uncontrolled) tremors in patients suffering the debilitating symptoms of Parkinson's disease. In the long-term, some victims may benefit from the implantation of an electronic stimulator in the region of the brain that controls body movements.

Smallpox was eradicated several years ago through worldwide vaccination. Mass vaccination could resume immediately should this deadly virus ever be used by terrorists as a biological weapon.

As many as two million Americans suffering with bipolar disorder (manic-depression) and schizophrenia no longer have to be institutionalized and can instead function normally, thanks to a variety of new, long-acting anti-psychotic drug therapies.

Amblyopia, or "lazy eye," is a serious visual impairment resulting from inadequate eye use in early childhood. It affects up to three percent of the general population and can lead to blindness if not treated in its early stages. In severe cases, surgical intervention may be required to restore proper vision.

Each year renal dialysis, a procedure that removes toxic waste products from the blood stream, extends the lives of more than 300,000 patients with end-stage kidney failure.

Carefully planned treatment regimens with anti-epileptic drugs can control up to 70 percent of recurrent seizures in the 3 million children and adults living with epilepsy.

Malaria is a chronic, sometimes fatal disease caused by a parasite that is transmitted to humans by mosquitoes. A new generation of drugs has been developed to fight the most severe forms of this disease, which can kill up to two million people each year. New anti-malarial agents have been developed to protect military personnel and other travelers in malaria-endemic areas.

Drugs that effectively shrink cancerous tumors (anti-angiogenesis) by cutting off their blood supply are being used to treat lymphomas and other discrete types of cancers.

The lives of thousands of kidney, liver and heart transplant recipients were prolonged and enhanced thanks to surgical advances and the development of effective immunosuppressive drugs that prevent organ rejection.

Fast-acting medications have significantly reduced the risk of death of patients suffering from heart attacks, asthma, and other allergenic diseases.

Improvements in antibiotic therapy have helped extend the lives and improve the lung function of some 30,000 young people with cystic fibrosis, a deadly congestive lung disease.

Artificial blood substitutes are being developed for transfusions to save the lives of trauma patients in emergencies as well as those undergoing lengthy, complex surgical procedures.

Between 70 and 85 percent of the 5.5 million stroke survivors in the USA have no permanent disability thanks to the discovery of anti-coagulants and thrombolytic agents that prevent and dissolve potentially fatal blood clots.

Almost 38 million Americans should take a wide variety of new cholesterol-lowering drugs to prevent plaque buildup and reduce the incidence of heart attack, stroke and kidney failure.

From the rapidly growing field of biotechnology, DNA recombination made possible the sequencing of the human genome and laid the field for the new fields of nanomedicine and individualized therapy.

[Because of animal research] new surgical techniques to repair heart defects are being developed.

As human genes and their functions are identified, the relatively new technique of gene transfer offers a new strategy for treating diseases of genetic origin. The procedure involves inserting a normal gene to replace an "abnormal gene" in a target cell. Scientists are in the early stages of applying this method to treat such diseases as Huntington's chorea, hemophilia, sickle cell anemia, cystic fibrosis and certain types of cancer. The ultimate goal of Human Genome Project research is to characterize all human genetic material (DNA) to understand the working of biological systems.

Teams of scientists are now identifying the therapeutic potential for transplanting both embryonic and adult stem cells for a wide range of therapies in such devastating diseases as cancer, Alzhiemer's and Parkinson's disease.

Advanced Surgical Interventions

Open heart surgery—coronary artery bypass, valve replacement and repair of congenital defects—is becoming common practice. In many cases, patients can return to normal daily activities.

Most of the 400,000 patients who undergo successful hip and knee replacements each year no longer face confinement in wheelchairs and experience less pain when walking.

New surgical techniques to repair heart defects are being developed to help the approximately 40,000 infants who are born with congenital abnormalities each year.

Thanks to recent advances in ophthalmologic surgery, more than 1.5 million Americans undergo cataract removal in a simple out-patient procedure that prevents vision loss.

15

Animal Experimentation Hampers Medical Research

Pat Thomas

Pat Thomas is health editor of the Ecologist, *a British newsmagazine with an ecological perspective.*

Animal experimentation does not work. Unfortunately, scientists have relied on these tests, and as a result, many of the drugs approved through animal experimentation have proven dangerous to humans. In order to make experimentation more accurate, scientists should rely on human cells and carefully conducted clinical trials with humans. Unfortunately, many scientists continue to rely on animal experimentation, which equals bargain basement medicine. Furthermore, animal rights activists who argue for the ethical rights of animals sidestep the central point: ethical or not, animal experimentation does not work. In essence, animal experimentation cannot predict many of the dangerous side effects caused by new products (drugs, cosmetics, and so on). Still, the pharmaceutical and cosmetic industries rely on these experiments to prevent future lawsuits. Animal experimentation may have even prolonged the emergence of many medical cures: by relying on animal research, scientists failed to explore other methods. Finally, good solutions will require good science, a process that will focus on producing a few good drugs that truly work.

Pat Thomas, "Animal Testing—Dangerous to Human Health," *WDDTY, What Doctors Don't Tell You*, accessed August 1, 2008. Reproduced by permission.

Overwhelming evidence demonstrates that animal tests are dangerous to human health, and may be the reason that so many 'safety tested' drugs cause so many side effects.

Animal testing doesn't work.

Its results are often inconclusive and cannot be accurately extrapolated to humans. As a result, relying on the results of animal testing can be dangerous to human health. It is a system which is long overdue for a critical review and yet no such review is on the horizon.

In his seminal book, the *Naked Empress: The Great Medical Fraud* . . . eminent researcher Hans Ruesch notes that approximately 15,000 new drugs are marketed every year, while some 12,000 are withdrawn. According to the Food and Drug Administration (FDA). 1.5 million Americans were hospitalised in 1978 alone as a consequence of pharmaceutical drugs administered to "cure" them. A further 30 per cent of all hospitalised people suffered further damage from the therapy prescribed to them. In the 1990s, studies show that 180,000 medically induced deaths occur each year in the USA. . . . Of course a percentage of these are due to incorrect prescription and administration of drugs but it still begs the question: how safe are the "safety tested" drugs we use?

Although our scientists argue that there are no real alternatives, this attitude is changing. To be helpful to human beings, drugs should be tested using human tissues, cells and organs (known as in vitro cultures). Chromatography and mass spectrometry, which separate drug substances at their molecular level to identify their properties, and quantum pharmacology, using quantum mechanics to understand the molecular structure of chemicals are also viable means of testing drugs.

Bargain Basement Medicine

More importantly, properly carried out human clinical trials and thorough reporting of drug side effects by post marketing surveillance are urgently needed. The AMES (in vitro test used to identify the presence of toxins) test used in conjunction with other in vitro tests can be very effective in determining carcinogenic (cancer causing) and teratogenic (ability to cause birth defects) properties of substances. And yet these methods are not widely used. Consequently, researchers are unfamiliar with them and resistant to the idea of new training. Because they are not widely used, they are more expensive. Because they are more expensive, they are not widely funded. The truth is that animal testing is the bargain basement of medicine. And we're getting what we pay for.

To counter this situation, many committed organisations have tried to alert the public to what is first and foremost the inhumanity of these tests. However, it is doubtful whether, in a culture that doesn't take the concept of human rights all that seriously, the concept of animal rights will ever be given much priority. Under the very broad umbrella of "animal rights", there are now groups who believe that, by clinging to the idea of animals' moral rights and using methods of emotional blackmail or even outright violence to get its message across, the movement has continually shot itself in the foot. These few argue that in a climate which is increasingly calling for evidence based medicine, the case for what is known as the "three Rs" reducing, refining and replacing animal testing can be convincingly argued and won through levelheaded analysis of the scientific research.

There is no doubt that there is copious evidence from the fields of vaccination, cancer, heart disease, stomach ulcers and sudden infant death to show that animal testing does not work. That more scientists and medical researchers have not cottoned on to this fact is surprising. Indeed, the debates in the medical press have been lacklustre to say the least, with pro vivisectionists relying on tradition . . . heroism . . . and even paranoia. . . .

Anti vivisectionists, on the other hand, have tried to remain levelheaded in print to an extent that they fail to make their point forcefully enough. . . . A few, like Dr Peter Mansfield, president of Doctors in Britain Against Animal Experiments, speak plainly: "The pharmaceutical industry has products to sell and under the law as it stands needs animal experiments to help them do it. They say we need animal experiments for the advancement of medical science, but it is the future of their industry that really concerns them."

Many of the most common life threatening side effects of drugs cannot be predicted by animal tests.

To date, much of the most convincing evidence against animal testing has been independently compiled by antivivisectionist individuals and groups. There remains, however, a long standing difficulty in trying to get research which contradicts the current enthusiasm for animal testing published in major medical journals. Whether this is through the diffidence of the major publishers, which are forced by commercial concerns to consent to and uphold these views, is unclear.

A quick flick through any major journal shows that as surely as women's magazines rely on advertising from cosmetics companies, medical journals rely on the advertising money of major pharmaceutical companies. This will have a bearing on the vetting system for research articles. As a result, much of the evidence ends up in books and newsletters.

The Poor Predictability of Animal Testing

Many of the most common life threatening side effects of drugs cannot be predicted by animal tests. Animals, for instance, cannot let the experimenter know if they are suffering from headache, amnesia, nausea, depression and other psychological disturbances. Allergic reactions, some blood disorders, skin lesions and many central nervous system effects are even more serious examples that cannot be demonstrated by animal models.

Given the large variety of laboratory animals available, and the widely varying laboratory conditions under which experiments are carried out, it should come as no surprise that the results of animal testing can be used to prove or disprove almost anything. Indeed it is this "flexibility" of animal testing which makes it so appealing to researchers and drug companies. . . .

A . . . bizarre example is the drug tamoxifen, used to treat human breast cancer by blocking the production of oestrogen. Although tamoxifen reduces the incidence of mammary cancer in rodents, it actually increases the incidence of liver cancer in them. . . . From these studies, one would conclude that the drug is toxic to the kidneys. However, in human subjects, tamoxifen has been shown to cause uterine cancer. . . . Studies put the risk in humans between two and six times that of controls.

The Limits of Animal Testing

Although the stated rationale behind animal testing is that it is done for the greater good of mankind, there is a strong argument that really it is done for legal rather than scientific reasons. Performing the necessary animal experimentation serves as a legal alibi for corporations when their products damage or kill those who use them.

Thalidomide recently reapproved by the FDA, is a classic example. During the lengthy trial of the manufacturers in 1970, numerous court witnesses, all animal experimenters, stated under oath that the results of animal experiments are never 100 per cent valid for human beings. However because the manufacturers performed the required animal safety tests, and because these tests did not show any evidence of danger, the manufacturers of thalidomide were found not guilty by the court of consciously making a harmful drug.

As Robert Sharpe points out, "In pregnant animals, differences in the physiological structure, function and biochemistry of the placenta aggravate the usual differences in metabolism, excretion, distribution and absorption that exists between species and make reliable predictions impossible." In the animal testing of thalidomide, the grotesque malformations caused by the drug in humans proved impossible to replicate.

In his book *Drugs as Teratogens*, J.L. Scharden comments: "In approximately 10 strains of rats, 15 strains of mice, eleven breeds of rabbit, two breeds of dogs, three strains of hamsters, eight species of primates and in other such varied species as cats, armadillos, guinea pigs, swine and ferrets in which thalidomide has been tested, teratogenic effects have been induced only occasionally."

After the trial, the animal testing lobby tried to say that thalidomide was a "rare exception" and that this tragedy "emphasises a need for more rigorous animal testing, not less."

Inconsistent Results

Medical historian Hans Ruesch takes up the story in his own book: "Only when the white New Zealand rabbit was tested, a few malformed rabbit babies were obtained, and subsequently also some malformed monkeys after years of tests (with increasing doses), hundreds of different strains and millions of dead animals used. But researchers immediately pointed out that malformations, like cancer, could be obtained by administration of practically any substance in high concentration, including sugar and salt, which will eventually upset the organism, causing trouble."

Animal testing also has an abysmal record in developing useful drugs to combat the effects of stroke. Following experiments on rabbits, dogs, gerbils and monkeys, animal researchers suggested that barbiturates could protect against the effects of stroke. In human stroke victims, however, barbiturates had little or no protective effect. By contrast the drug nimodipine has shown some effect on specific kinds of stroke namely sub arachnoid haemorrhage (though not without several unpleasant side effects such as hypotension, headache and nausea). But the animal data on the drug are inconsistent and conflicting; in cats and baboons, for instance, nimodipine produced no overall beneficial effect. Today, we know that gastric ulcers are mainly caused by the bacteria *Helicobactor pylori*. However, use of animal models to develop effective drug treatment may have delayed this discovery by as much as 100 years.

There is an alternative to animal research and it's called good science.

For decades, building on experiments of the gastric secretions of dogs, researchers began cutting the vagus nerve to treat stomach ulcer patients. It was believed that if the acid in digestive juice could be reduced, ulcers would be cured. This theory flew in the face of the knowledge, even in the late 19th century, that the digestive action of the stomach lay in an enzyme called pepsin, and not in acid itself.

Sometime after the 1940s, the role of the vagus nerve of animals was soon discovered to be different from humans, especially dogs the very species on which the technique was originally developed. Nevertheless experimentation continued, and the canine model, and eventually its equivalent in rats, was used to develop drugs which would reduce stomach acid secretions. These drugs include those acting upon the histamine system, such as cimetidine or the proton pump inhibitors like omeprazole, which act upon another stomach enzyme. It took until the 1980s for researchers to discover the *H pylori* bacterial connection.

False Patterns of Disease

The fact that the laboratory animal is relatively healthy before the experiment means that disease and or trauma has to be induced by artificial and often violent means. This bears no relation whatsoever to the spontaneous ways in which humans develop illness, often through faulty lifestyle and diet.

Consider the case of osteoarthritis, a human degenerative disease resulting in painful deformities of the joints. In order to mimic human lameness in dogs, cats, sheep and pigs, researchers beat the joints of animals with hammer blows, inject them with irritating liquids, subject them to ionising radiation and/or dislocate them. Of course, the resulting fractures, haemorrhages, thromboses, confusions) and inflammations bear no relation to human osteoarthritis. Drugs which are then tested on such artificially diseased, non human animals cannot possibly yield results relevant to a spontaneously occurring human disease.

Better Drugs, Not More Drugs

Clearly we don't need as many drugs as there are in the marketplace. Indeed, in 1981, the United Nations Industrial Development Organisation in collaboration with the WHO [World Health Organisation], published a list of only 26 drugs, from the 205,000 on the market, which were considered "indispensable", with nine of these being considered more indispensable than others.

According to Peter Mansfield, it is "by luck, rather than good judgement" that we have, over the past thirty years, stumbled upon many useful drugs which have a known range of safety and danger, and which "will continue to be used in appropriate and well defined circumstances." But while there will be a continued need for drugs, Mansfield envisages a day when the whole paradigm of medical care will change.

"Science is really a method for answering questions. If we ask a stupid question, scientific methods will faithfully produce for us a stupid answer. We must debate carefully, therefore, what questions we ask our scientists to tackle.

"The drug industry can be relied on to ask for the best drug solution to each medical problem. We must broaden the question: what is the best solution overall? Sometimes it may be a drug, more usually not. A drug may relieve the pain and inflammation of displaced muscles and joints, but only a manipulative treatment stands any chance of curing it. Diet offers major benefits in dealing with rheumatism, which drugs cannot improve in the long run. The likelihood is that drugs will retain a major part in the first aid treatment of many diseases, but that other methods will offer better chances of long term benefit and prevention of relapse."

There is an alternative to animal research and it's called good science.

Organizations to Contact

The editors have compiled the following list of organizations concerned with the issues debated in this book. The descriptions are derived from materials provided by the organizations. All have publications or information available for interested readers. The list was compiled on the date of publication of the present volume; the information provided here may change. Be aware that many organizations take several weeks or longer to respond to inquiries, so allow as much time as possible.

American Anti-Vivisection Society (AAVS)
801 Old York Road, Suite 204, Jenkintown, PA   19046-1685
(215) 887-0816 • fax: (215) 887-2088
e-mail: aavs@aavs.org
Web site: www.aavs.org

AAVS advocates the abolition of vivisection, opposes all types of experiments on living animals, and sponsors research on alternatives to these methods. The society produces videos and publishes numerous brochures as well as the award-winning *AV Magazine* whose issues are each dedicated to a different topic concerning animals, such as vivisection in education and animal testing alternatives.

American Association for Laboratory Animal Science (AALAS)
9190 Crestwyn Hills Drive, Memphis, TN   38125-8538
(901) 754-8620 • fax: (901) 753-0046
e-mail: info@aalas.org
Web site: www.aalas.org

AALAS collects and exchanges information on all aspects of the management, care, and procurement of laboratory animals. Its publications include *AALAS in Action* and *Contemporary Topics in Laboratory Animal Science*.

American Society for the Prevention of Cruelty to Animals (ASPCA)

424 E. Ninety-second St., New York, NY   10128-6804
(212) 876-7700 • fax: (212) 348-3031
e-mail: press@aspca.org
Web site: www.aspca.org

The ASPCA promotes appreciation for and humane treatment of animals, encourages enforcement of anticruelty laws, and works for the passage of legislation that strengthens existing animal protection laws. In addition to making available books, brochures, and videos on animal issues, the ASPCA publishes *Animal Watch*, a quarterly magazine.

Animal Legal Defense Fund (ALDF)

170 East Cotati Ave., Cotati, CA   94931
(707) 795-2533 • fax: (707) 795-7280
e-mail: info@aldf.org
Web site: www.aldf.org

ALDF is an organization of attorneys and law students who promote animal rights and protect the lives and interests of animals through the use of their legal skills. It publishes the *Animals' Advocate* quarterly.

AnimalScam

Center for Consumer Freedom, Washington, DC   20038
Web site: www.animalscam.com

AnimalScam is a project of the Center for Consumer Freedom, a nonprofit organization that promotes personal responsibility and protects consumers' choices. AnimalScam refutes claims made by animal rights activists, reveals what it says are hidden agendas of animal rights groups, and protects the rights of Americans to eat meat, drink milk, wear fur, and visit zoos. News articles, quotes by animal rights activists, and anti–animal rights groups' ads are posted on its Web site.

Animal Welfare Institute (AWI)
PO Box 3650, Washington, DC   20007
(703) 836-4300 • fax: (703) 836-0400
e-mail: awi@animalwelfare.com
Web site: www.animalwelfare.com

The Animal Welfare Institute is a nonprofit charitable organization founded in 1951 to reduce the sum total of pain and fear inflicted on animals by humans. It advocates the humane treatment of laboratory animals and the development and use of nonanimal testing methods as well as encourages humane science teaching and prevention of painful experiments on animals by high school students. The AWI publications include the books *Beyond the Laboratory Door* and *The Principles of Humane Experimental Technique,* and the newsletter *AWI Quarterly.*

Foundation for Biomedical Research (FBR)
818 Connecticut Ave. NW, Ste. 900, Washington, DC   20006
(202) 457-0654 • fax: (202) 457-0659
e-mail: info@fbresearch.org
Web site: www.fbresearch.org

FBR provides informational and educational programs about what it sees as the necessary and important role of laboratory animals in biomedical research and testing. Its videos include *Waiting for a Cure* and *Caring for Life.* It also publishes a newsletter, *Foundation for Biomedical Research.*

Fund for Animals
200 W. Fifty-seventh St., New York, NY   10019
toll-free: (888) 405-FUND • fax: (212) 246-2633
e-mail: fundinfo@fund.org
Web site: www.fund.org

The Fund for Animals encourages children and adults to deal with animals more humanely. It publicizes animal protection issues, facilitates the passage of pro-animal legislation, and helps to stave off bills that allow animals to be exploited or harmed. Numerous fact sheets, press releases, and reports are available on its Web site, as is a link to free subscriptions of its quarterly newspaper for teens, *Animal Free Press*.

The Great Ape Project (GAP)
806A NW Fifty-first St., Seattle, WA   98107
(206) 579-5975
e-mail: info@greatapeproject.org
Web site: www.greatapeproject.org

GAP, an international organization, works to include great apes within the category of persons. It believes that due to their humanlike mental capacities and emotions, great apes deserve the same basic moral and legal rights as people enjoy. GAP publishes a free newsletter called *GAP News*; its books include *The Great Ape Project: Equality Beyond Humanity* and *The Great Ape Project Census*.

Humane Society of the United States (HSUS)
2100 L St. NW, Washington, DC   20037
(202) 452-1100 • fax: (202) 778-6132
Web site: www.hsus.org

HSUS works to foster respect, understanding, and compassion for all creatures. Among its many diverse efforts, it maintains programs supporting responsible pet ownership and the elimination of cruelty in hunting and trapping. It also exposes painful uses of animals in research and testing and abusive treatment of animals in movies, circuses, pulling contests, and racing. It campaigns for animal protection legislation and monitors the enforcement of existing animal protection statutes. HSUS publishes the quarterlies *All Animals* and *HSUS News*.

Institute of Laboratory Animal Research (ILAR)
The National Academies, Washington, DC   20001
(202) 334-2590 • fax: (202) 334-1687
e-mail: ILAR@nas.edu
Web site: http://dels.nas.edu/ilar_n/ilarhome/

Organized under the auspices of the National Academy of Sciences, ILAR advises, upon request, the federal government and other agencies concerning the use of animals in biomedical research. It prepares guidelines and policy papers on biotechnology, the use of animals in precollege education, and other topics in laboratory animal science. Its publications include *Guide for the Care and Use of Laboratory Animals* and the quarterly *ILAR News.*

Institute for In Vitro Sciences (IIVS)
Institute for In Vitro Sciences, Gaithersburg, MD   20878
(301) 947-6523 • fax: (301) 947-6538
Web site: www.iivs.org

IIVS is a nonprofit, technology-driven, foundation for the advancement of alternative methods to animal testing. In order to facilitate the reduction of animal use in testing, the institute promotes the optimization, use, and acceptance of in vitro methodologies worldwide. IIVS makes its published articles available on its Web site.

**Johns Hopkins Center for Alternatives to Animal
Testing (CAAT)**
111 Market Place, Suite 840, Baltimore, MD   21202-6709
(410) 223-1693 • fax: (410) 223-1603
e-mail: caat@jhsph.edu
Web site: http://caat.jhsph.edu

CAAT fosters the development of scientifically acceptable alternatives to animal testing for use in creating and evaluating the safety of commercial and therapeutic products. The center conducts symposia for researchers and corporations. One of its publications is *Animals and Alternatives in Testing: History, Science, and Ethics.*

Medical Research Modernization Committee (MRMC)
3200 Morley Road, Shaker Heights, OH   44122
(216) 283-6702 • fax: (216) 283-6702
Web site: www.mrmcmed.org

The MRMC is a national health advocacy group composed of physicians, scientists, and other health-care professionals who evaluate benefits, risks, and costs of medical research methods and technologies. The MRMC attributes the steadily increasing incidence of cancer, AIDS, and other uniquely human diseases to inadequate treatment approaches derived from research programs based on artificial and unnatural laboratory "models." Its publications include the quarterly *MRMC Report* and *A Critical Look at Animal Experimentation.*

National Animal Interest Alliance (NAIA)
PO Box 66579, Portland, OR   97290-6579
(503) 761-1139
e-mail: editor@naiaonline.org
Web site: www.naiaonline.org

The National Animal Interest Alliance is an educational rather than an activist organization. The goal of the NAIA is to provide balancing information and services where animal rights activities or other forms of animal exploitation have diverted attention from facts and foundational issues. In this capacity NAIA serves as a clearinghouse for information and as an access point for subject matter experts, keynote speakers, and issue analysis. *NAIA News* is the organization's newspaper.

People for the Ethical Treatment of Animals (PETA)
501 Front St., Norfolk, VA   23510
(757) 622-PETA (7382) • fax: (757) 622-0457
e-mail: peta@norfolk.infi.net
Web site: www.peta.org/

An international animal rights organization, PETA is dedicated to establishing and protecting the rights of all animals. It focuses on four areas: factory farms, research laboratories, the fur trade, and the entertainment industry. PETA promotes public education, cruelty investigations, animal rescue, celebrity involvement, and legislative action. It produces numerous videos and publishes the children's magazine *Animal Times, Grrr!* as well as various fact sheets, brochures, flyers, and a weekly e-newsletter.

Uncaged Campaigns
5th Fl., Alliance House, 9 Leopold St., Sheffield S1 2GY
  UK
+44 114 272 2220
e-mail: info@uncaged.co.uk
Web site: www.uncaged.co.uk/

Uncaged Campaigns works to end vivisection and to ascribe moral and legal rights to animals. It is best known for winning a legal battle to release *Diaries of Despair*, the animal transplantation reports of Huntingdon Life Sciences, a commercial research company that Uncaged Campaigns accuses of breaching animal welfare practices. Members receive *Uncaged!*, its quarterly newsmagazine.

Zoocheck Canada
788 ½ O'Connor Dr., Toronto, ON
  M4B 2S6
(416) 285-1744 • fax: (416) 285-4670
e-mail: zoocheck@zoocheck.com
Web site: www.zoocheck.com

Zoocheck Canada aims to protect animals' welfare through investigation, research, campaigns, and legal actions. Many of the news articles and reports on its Web site discuss animal welfare across the globe, including in the United States, Central and South America, and the United Kingdom. It produces videos, audiotapes, and reports about animal rights issues as well as a quarterly newsletter, *Natural Justice*, about animals and Canadian law.

Bibliography

Books

Robert M. Baird and Stuart E. Rosenbaum, eds. *Animal Experimentation: The Moral Issues*. Buffalo, NY: Prometheus, 1991.

Luigi Boitani and Todd Fuller, eds. *Research Techniques in Animal Ecology*. New York: Columbia University Press, 2000.

Colin Burgess and Chris Dubbs *Animals in Space: From Research Rockets to the Space Shuttle*. New York: Springer, 2007.

Larry Carbone *What Animals Want: Expertise and Advocacy in Laboratory Animal Welfare Policy*. New York: Oxford University Press, 2004.

Marilyn E. Carroll and J. Bruce Overmier, eds. *Animal Research and Human Health: Advancing Human Welfare Through Behavioral Science*. Washington, DC: American Psychological Association, 2001.

P. Michael Conn and James V. Parker *The Animal Research War*. New York: Palgrave Macmillan, 2008.

Nancy Day *Animal Experimentation: Cruelty or Science?* Berkeley Heights, NJ: Enslow, 2000.

Alix Fano   *Lethal Laws: Animal Testing, Human Health and Environmental Policy.* New York: Zed, 1997.

Jean Swingle Greek and C. Ray Greek   *What Will We Do If We Don't Experiment on Animals?* Victoria, BC: Trafford, 2006.

Hugh LaFollette   *Brute Science: Dilemmas of Animal Experimentation.* New York: Routledge, 1997.

Randall Lockwood and Frank R. Ascione, eds.   *Cruelty to Animals and Interpersonal Violence: Readings in Research and Application.* West Lafayette, IN: Purdue University Press, 1998.

Vaughan Monamy   *Animal Experimentation: A Guide to the Issues.* New York: Cambridge University Press, 2000.

Bernard E. Rollin   *Animal Rights and Human Morality.* Amherst, NY: Prometheus, 2006.

Harry Salem, ed.   *Advances in Animal Alternatives for Safety and Efficacy Testing.* Washington, DC: Informa Healthcare, 1997.

Peter Singer, ed.   *In Defense of Animals: The Second Wave.* Malden, MA: Blackwell, 2006.

Periodicals

Bakersfield Californian   "Terrorists Targeting Researchers," August 28, 2008.

Thomas Barlow   "Paying for Knowledge with a Trail of Carcasses," *Financial Times*, July 7, 2001.

Choice   "Cosmetics: Safe and Cruelty-Free?" April 2006.

Choice   "Cruelty-Free Beauty," April 2006.

Chronicle of Higher Education   "New Front in Battle over Studies of Animals," June 27, 2008.

Randy Cohen   "Giving Art a Hand," *New Times*, October 12, 2003.

P. Michael Conn and James V. Parker   "Winners and Losers in the Animal-Research War," *American Scientist*, May/June 2008.

Current Events   "Monkey in the Middle," January 27, 2007.

Economist   "Humane League," September 1, 2007.

Europe Agri   "Research: New Solutions Expected to Cut Down on Animal Testing," April 30, 2007.

Global Agenda   "Dodging the Law," September 12, 2007.

Sally G. Hoskins   "Lessons in Life," *Newsweek*, June 16, 2008.

Information Week   "Robots, Computers to Help Phase Out Animal Testing," February 15, 2008.

Tanuja Koppal   "Chipping Away at Animal Testing,"
                       Bioscience Technology, April 2008.

Richard   "Protestors Fail to Slow Animal
Monastersky   Research," *Chronicle of Higher
                       Education*, April 18, 2008.

Nature   "Animal Tests Inescapable," May 29,
                       2008.

Jehangir Pocha   "Animal Tester," *Forbes*, October 30,
                       2006.

Jehangir Pocha   "Comparative Advantage," *Forbes*,
                       November 13, 2006.

Nick Price   "Hail Caesar," *Chemistry and
                       Industry*, August 11, 2008.

Andrew Read   "Vivisectionists Strike Back," *Nature*,
                       May 29, 2008.

Anne Riley-Katz   "Protesters Force Juice Maker to End
                       Testing on Animals," *Los Angeles
                       Business Journal*, January 22, 2007.

Sacramento (CA)   "Animals in Experiments," May 27,
Bee   2008.

Wesley J. Smith   "Human Guinea Pigs," *Weekly
                       Standard*, January 3, 2006.

Jo Tanner   "Standing Up for Animal Research,"
                       Chemistry and Industry, May 1, 2006.

Pamela S. Turner   "Are Ape Rights the Next Frontier?"
                       Odyssey, April 2008.

Rich Ulmer   "The Future of Safety Testing Labs,"
                    Global Cosmetic Industry, August
                    2007.

Meredith   "Medical Schools Swap Pigs for
Wadman   Plastic," *Nature*, May 8, 2008.

Index